D0098938

1542
V. 1

248.4899 Swindoll, Charles
SWI   R.

         Living beyond the
         daily grind

DEC 15 1988
$14.95

DATE			

STORAGE   1542
                           LT

San Diego Public Library

© THE BAKER & TAYLOR CO.

LIVING BEYOND THE DAILY GRIND

BOOK I

OTHER PUBLICATIONS BY CHARLES R. SWINDOLL

Books:

Come Before Winter
Compassion: Showing Care in a
  Careless World
Dropping Your Guard
Encourage Me
For Those Who Hurt
Growing Deep in the Christian
  Life
Growing Strong in the Seasons
  of Life
Growing Wise in Family Life
Hand Me Another Brick
Improving Your Serve
Killing Giants, Pulling Thorns
Leadership: Influence That
  Inspires

Living Above the Level of
  Mediocrity
Living on the Ragged Edge
Make Up Your Mind
The Quest for Character
Recovery: When Healing Takes
  Time
Standing Out
Starting Over
Strengthening Your Grip
Strike the Original Match
Three Steps Forward, Two Steps
  Back
Victory: A Winning Game Plan
  for Life
You and Your Child

Booklets:

Anger
Attitudes
Commitment
Dealing with Defiance
Demonism
Destiny
Divorce
Eternal Security
God's Will
Hope
Impossibilities
Integrity
Leisure

The Lonely Whine of the
  Top Dog
Moral Purity
Our Mediator
Peace in Spite of Panic
Prayer
Sensuality
Singleness
Stress
Tongues
When Your Comfort Zone Gets
  the Squeeze
Woman

Films:

People of Refuge
Strengthening Your Grip

CHARLES R. SWINDOLL

REFLECTIONS ON THE SONGS AND SAYINGS IN SCRIPTURE

LIVING BEYOND THE DAILY GRIND

BOOK I

WORD PUBLISHING

Dallas · London · Sydney · Singapore

LIVING BEYOND THE DAILY GRIND: REFLECTIONS ON THE SONGS
AND SAYINGS OF SCRIPTURE (BOOK I)

Copyright © 1988 by Charles R. Swindoll. All rights reserved. No portion of
this book may be reproduced in any form, except for brief quotations in
reviews, without written permission from the publisher.

Unless otherwise indicated, Scripture quotations used in this book are from
the New American Standard Bible, © 1960, 1962, 1963, 1968, 1971, 1972,
1973, 1975, 1977 by The Lockman Foundation. Used by permission.

Other Scripture quotations are from the following sources: The King James
Version of the Bible (KJV). The New Testament in Modern English (PHILLIPS) by
J. B. Phillips, published by The Macmillan Company, © 1958, 1960, 1972
by J. B. Phillips. The Amplified Bible (AMP). Copyright © 1965 Zondervan
Publishing House. *The Living Bible* (TLB), copyright 1971 by Tyndale House
Publishers, Wheaton, IL. Used by permission. The *Good News Bible,* Today's
English Version (TEV)—Old Testament: Copyright © American Bible Society
1976; New Testament: Copyright © American Bible Society 1966, 1971, 1976.
The Modern Language Bible (MLB), The Berkeley Version in Modern English.
Copyright © 1945, 1959, 1969 by Zondervan Publishing House. Used by per-
mission. The Holy Bible, New International Version (NIV). Copyright © 1973,
1978, 1984 International Bible Society. Used by permission of Zondervan
Bible Publishers.

Library of Congress Cataloging-in-Publication Data:

Swindoll, Charles R.
  Living beyond the daily grind.
  1. Bible. O.T. Psalms—Meditations. 2. Bible.
O.T. Proverbs—Meditations. 3. Christian life—
Biblical teaching. I. Title.
BS1430.4.S95 1988   248.4'899   88-20513
ISBN 0-8499-0654-7 (v. 1)
ISBN 0-8499-0673-3 (v. 2)

Printed in the United States of America

8 9 8 0 1 2 3 9 AGH 9 8 7 6 5 4 3 2 1

It is with deep feelings of gratitude that I dedicate this volume to the men who served on the faculty at Dallas Theological Seminary during my years of training from 1959 to 1963.

Their competent scholarship, insightful instruction, unfailing dedication to Christ as Lord, and relentless commitment to the Scriptures as the inerrant Word of God have marked me for life.

CONTENTS

INTRODUCTION

> Without a song the day would never end;
> Without a song the road would never bend;
> When things go wrong a man ain't got a friend,
> Without a song.
> . . . .
> I got my trouble and woe,
> But sure as I know the Jordan will roll,
> I'll get along as long as a song is strong
> In my soul. . . .[1]

Even though this song was composed before I was born (which makes it a *real* oldie), I often find myself returning to the tune. It slips out in places like my shower at the beginning of a busy day, between appointments and assignments in the middle of a hectic day, and on the road home at the end of a tiring day. Somehow it adds a touch of oil to the grind, smoothing things up a bit. Willie Nelson recently blew the dust off the old lyrics. I still sing them to myself . . .

> Without a song the day would never end;
> Without a song the road would never bend;
> When things go wrong a man ain't got a friend,
> Without a song.

True, isn't it? The right combination of words, melody, and rhythm seldom fails to work like magic. And given the pressures and demands folks like us are forced to cope with on a daily basis, we could use a little magic. Most of the people I know are never totally free of a relentless daily grind.

—The homemaker with ever-present children at her feet faces fourteen or more hours a day in the grind of meeting deadlines, making decisions, competing with strong wills, and completing an endless list of chores.

—The professional experiences a grind of a different type: people, people, people . . . especially dissatisfied people who would rather scream and sue than smile and solve, which only intensifies the drain brought on by increasing expectations and decreasing energy.

—The truck driver has an altogether different but equally exhausting routine: the grind of traffic snarls, weather hazards, thoughtless drivers, and monotonous miles.

—Then there is the grind of repetition the athlete must live with: unending hours of practice, weight training, road work, watching films, perfecting technique, fierce competition, injuries, loneliness, boredom, exhaustion . . . only to wake up to another day of the same song, fifth verse.

—And who can deny the exacting requirements of academic pursuits? Students and faculty alike must live with the ceaseless, cyclical grind of daily preparation and assignments, attending class, doing projects, choosing electives, cramming for exams, grading papers, and (hopefully) earning a degree or tenure.

Fact is, the grind is not going away! The salesperson has to live with a quota. The performer must constantly rehearse. The therapist can't escape one depressed soul after another. The pilot has to stay strapped in for hours. The preacher is never free of sermon preparation. The broadcaster cannot get away from the clock any more than the bureaucrat can escape the hassle of red tape. Days don't end . . . roads don't bend. . . . Help!

Instead of belaboring the point, since we cannot escape the grind, we must find a way to live beyond it. The question is, how? The answer is, a song. Remember? "Without a song the day would never end." But not just any song! Certainly not some mindless, earsplitting tune yelled at us by a bunch of weird-looking jerks with blue and orange hair, dressed in black leather and spikes, and microphones stuffed halfway down their throats. No, not that. I have in mind some songs that are really old. We're talking ancient. In fact, they are the ones inspired and composed by our Creator-God—the original Rock music with a capital *R.* They're called psalms.

These are timeless songs—that have yielded delicious fruit in every generation. They're not silly ditties, but strong, melodious messages written with life's daily grind in mind and specially designed to help us live beyond it. That's right, *beyond* it. To borrow again from the songwriter, "We'll get along as long as a *psalm* is strong in our souls." I really do believe that. Why else would God have inspired those age-old compositions? Surely, He realized the lasting value of each musical masterpiece and therefore preserved them to help us persevere. They drip with the oil of glory that enables us to live beyond the grind.

Along with the songs, Scripture provides us with wise sayings as well. David's brilliant son Solomon, the man of wisdom, left in his legacy one axiom after another which, when applied, gives us the wisdom we need to cope with life's daily grind. These sayings are known as proverbs.

Interestingly, the original term *proverbs* is a Latin derivative, meaning "to represent something." It conveys the thought of similarity: *pro,* meaning "for" or "in the place of" and *verba,* meaning "words." A proverb, therefore, is a statement in the place of many words . . . a crisp saying, briefly stated, given to regulate our lives. The Book of Proverbs is a rich treasure house of short sentences drawn from long experiences.

When they are woven into the fabric of our daily hassles, it is remarkable how much oil they add to our gears. And when these sayings are coupled with the songs in Scripture, who can possibly measure the benefits? The daily grind of life can be greatly reduced by an application of God's songs and sayings.

• Who hasn't been comforted, when frightened and alone, by the quiet reminder that "The Lord is my shepherd, / I shall not want"? Those are lyrics from an ancient song of David—Psalm 23.

• Who hasn't been calmed and refreshed from the reminder to "Trust in the Lord with all your heart, / And do not lean on your own understanding. / In all your ways acknowledge Him, / And He will make your paths straight"? Beautiful words! Wonderful words of life! They represent a saying from Solomon's inspired pen found in Proverbs 3.

• Again, who hasn't felt strangled by the grip of guilt . . . only to find soothing relief from "Be gracious to me, O God, according to Thy lovingkindness; / According to the greatness of Thy compassion blot out my transgressions / . . . Wash me, and I shall be whiter than snow"? Another song of David, hymn 51.

• And, again, who hasn't felt the finger of God pushing against his sternum when reading off the seven things the Lord hates: "Haughty eyes, a lying tongue, / And hands that shed innocent blood, / A heart that devises wicked plans, / Feet that run rapidly to evil, / A false witness who utters lies, / And one who spreads strife . . ."? Talk about a powerful saying! Solomon wrote it in Proverbs 6.

I could go on for pages. In fact, that is exactly what I intend to do! Since God's Book is full of such songs and sayings, I am convinced it is worth our while to spend our time pondering and applying these wise words and timeless principles.

To help make them stick, let's not try to digest too great a meal in one sitting. Seems to me these songs and sayings are like rich food, to be eaten slowly. Too much, too fast would be counterproductive. I realize the grinds we live with are of a daily nature . . . but I'm suggesting that we deal with each one on a weekly basis. That is why I have provided fifty-two songs and sayings in this two-volume set rather than three hundred sixty-five of them.

Let me urge you to take your time . . . to read each section carefully . . . to give your mind time to digest each weekly provision slowly . . . and to enter into my reflections methodically and meaningfully. I have kept the twenty-six readings in each volume practical and in touch with very real issues, which I have called daily grinds. I have also alternated the songs and sayings, using two thirteen-week segments of each to make sure we maintain a balance between the two throughout our fifty-two-week year.

Let's sing David's song through each day of the week. Let's also remember Solomon's saying with equal commitment. I believe these time-tested lyrics and axioms will add just enough oil to our days to enable us to live beyond the daily grind. Otherwise, our long days would never end and the wearisome road before us would never bend. How grateful I am for these inspired songs and sayings!

Before getting under way, I must pause and express my gratitude to Kip Jordon and Ernie Owen of Word Books. These men have become more than distant, professional associates in the publishing business. They are my friends whose sincere affirmation fuels my fire. Along with them I thank Beverly Phillips, my editor. Her careful attention to detail has been of inestimable value. And then I also want to mention Helen Peters, who has worked alongside me with each of my books. As a secretary she has no equal in diligence or in commitment.

If my numbering is correct, *Living Beyond the Daily Grind* is my twenty-fifth book . . . a milestone in my twelve-year publishing career. Words fail me as I attempt to describe the depth of my gratitude to my family for their understanding, their unselfishness, and their encouragement. Without their willingness to adapt to my writing addiction; to listen patiently to my incessant reading of what I have written; to prod me on during the dry spells; and to tolerate the late-night, middle-of-the-night, and early-morning flashes of insight that kept the light burning over the desk in my home study—there is no way I could have reached this milestone.

And now . . . let's press on. The year stretches out in front of us, and God's insightful songs and sayings await our appropriation. My desire is that this year of study and reflection of His Word will enable us to do more than plod along a tiresome path. If my weekly game plan works, we'll soon be living beyond the daily grind.

Chuck Swindoll
Fullerton, California

The Songs In Scripture

WEEK 1
THROUGH
WEEK 13

How blessed is the man who
does not walk in the counsel
of the wicked,
Nor stand in the path of
sinners,
Nor sit in the seat of scoffers!
But his delight is in the law of the Lord,
And in His law he meditates day and
night.
And he will be like a tree firmly planted
by streams of water,
Which yields its fruit in its season,
And its leaf does not wither;
And in whatever he does, he prospers.

The wicked are not so,
But they are like chaff which the wind
drives away.
Therefore the wicked will not stand in
the judgment,
Nor sinners in the assembly of the
righteous.
For the Lord knows the way of the
righteous,
But the way of the wicked will
perish.   [1:1–6]

THE GRIND OF COMPROMISE

One of the best-loved portions of God's Book is the Psalms. For centuries these songs have comforted, calmed, and consoled the hearts of readers. We shall turn to them during the first thirteen weeks of our journey together for the purpose of having our lives enriched by being exposed to their lyrics. Our interest is primarily a devotional one. We shall seek first to know the meaning of the psalm, and then grasp the practical significance of that psalm in light of some daily grind all of us must cope with. I will conclude each reading with a section entitled Reflections . . . which will include three practical suggestions to help you apply the oil of Scripture to that particular grind.

The Hebrews' ancient hymnal begins with a song that addresses one of life's most common grinds—compromise. Please understand, I'm not referring to those give-and-take times so necessary for living in harmony with one another. Without that healthy kind of compromise, nations could never find a meeting ground for peaceful coexistence. Furthermore, growing family members would seldom enjoy the freedom involved in giving one another room to be different were it not for the tolerance such compromise encourages.

I'm thinking, rather, of compromising with wrong . . . allowing the slow-moving tentacles of evil to wrap themselves around us, squeezing the joys and rewards of obedience from our lives. It happens so silently, so subtly, we hardly realize it's taking place. Like an enormous oak that has decayed for years from within then suddenly falls, those who permit the eroding grind of compromise can expect an ultimate collapse.

Years ago I recall reading of the construction of a city hall and fire station in a small northern Pennsylvania community. All the citizens were so proud of their new red brick structure—a long-awaited dream come true. Not too many weeks after moving in, however, strange things began to happen. Several doors failed to shut completely and a few windows wouldn't slide open very easily. As time passed, ominous cracks began to appear in the walls. Within a few months, the front door couldn't be locked since the foundation had shifted, and the roof began to leak. By and by, the little building that was once the source of great civic pride had to be condemned. An intense investigation revealed that deep mining blasts several miles away caused underground shock waves which subsequently weakened the earth beneath the building foundation, resulting in its virtual self-destruction.

So it is with compromise in a life. Slowly, almost imperceptibly, one rationalization leads to another, which triggers a series of equally damaging alterations in a life that was once stable, strong and reliable. That seems to be the concern of the psalmist as he composes his first song which encourages us to resist even the slightest temptation to compromise our convictions.

OUTLINE

Next to the Twenty-third Psalm, the First Psalm is perhaps the most familiar. It is brief and simple, direct and profound. Even a casual reading of these six verses leads us to see that it is filled with contrasts between two different walks of life—the godly and the ungodly. A simple yet acceptable outline of Psalm 1 would be:

  I. The Godly Life (vv. 1–3)
 II. The Ungodly Life (vv. 4–6)

Written between the lines of this ancient song is evidence of the age-old battle in which all of us are engaged: compromise— the erosion of our good intentions.

THE GODLY LIFE

In the first three verses the psalmist describes the one who chooses to live a righteous life . . . who consciously resists the subtle inroads of compromise that erode commitment to a godly life. He begins in verse 1 by illustrating (with three negatives) the importance of allowing absolutely no compromise with evil, lest the evil become a habit of life. Then, in verse 2, he shows the positive side of godliness and the means by which it may be attained, followed in verse 3 with a description of what results when a righteous walk is practiced. Now let's do some in-depth analysis:

> How blessed is the man who does not walk in the counsel of the
> wicked,
> Nor stand in the path of sinners,
> Nor sit in the seat of scoffers! [v. 1]

The first word, *blessed*, is somewhat bland in our English language. The Hebrew term is much more descriptive, especially with its plural ending. Perhaps a workable rendering would be, "Oh, the happiness, many times over. . . . "

What is it that causes such an abundance of happiness? It is the uncompromising purity of a righteous walk with God. We see this by analyzing the three categories of remaining terms in this verse.

walk	counsel	ungodly
stand	path	sinners
sit	seat	scoffers

The psalmist has spiritual erosion in mind. The word pictures give us the concept of how easy it is for our intentions toward righteousness to slow to a standstill or a complete stop as they are worn away by the company we choose to keep.

Walk

Walk is a term that suggests passing by or "a casual movement along the way." With its entire phrase, it implies the idea of one who does not imitate or "go through the casual motions" of wickedness. The word translated *counsel* comes from the Hebrew term meaning "hard, firm." Here, it means a definite, firm, planned direction. Consider this paraphrase of verse 1:

> Oh the happiness, many times over, of the one who does not even casually go through the motions or imitate the plan of life of those who live in ungodliness. . . .

It is not uncommon to flirt with the wicked life, periodically imitating the motions of one without Christ. We may, in jest, refer to the fun and excitement of ungodliness—or chuckle at our children's questionable actions. David warns us against that. He tells us that we will be abundantly more happy if we steer clear of anything that could give the erosion of spiritual compromise a head start.

Stand

The Hebrew word for *stand* has the idea of coming and taking one's stand. The word *path* comes from the word meaning "a marked-out path, a certain and precise way of life." Can you see the progressive deterioration toward more involvement in sinful living? The casual passerby slows down and before you know it, he takes his stand.

On the other hand, by taking a firm stand for righteousness, we will be "like a tree firmly planted by streams of water"— one that cannot be eroded by the winds of wickedness and unrighteousness.

Sit

The next word the psalmist emphasizes is *sit*. This suggests a permanent settling down, an abiding, even a permanent dwelling. It is made even clearer by the use of *seat*, meaning "habitation" or "permanent residence." Don't miss this: The way of life is in the sphere of "the scornful," the one who continually makes light of that which is sacred—the blasphemous crowd.

Can you see the picture in the writer's mind? We shall be happy many times over if we maintain a pure walk, free from even the slightest flirtation with evil. If we begin to "walk" in "the counsel of the wicked," it is easy to slip slowly into the habitation of the scornful. Three illustrations from the Bible flash into my mind. Two men flirted with evil, then fell; but there was one other who refused to begin a "walk in the way of the ungodly."

The first two I'm thinking of are Lot and Samson, and the third is Joseph. People the world over are familiar with Samson, whose life is best described in Proverbs 5:20–23:

> For why should you, my son, be exhilarated with an adulteress,
> And embrace the bosom of a foreigner?
> For the ways of a man are before the eyes of the Lord,
> And He watches all his paths.
> His own iniquities will capture the wicked,
> And he will be held with the cords of his sin.
> He will die for lack of instruction,
> And in the greatness of his folly he will go astray.

Most people are not as well-acquainted with Lot, Abraham's nephew. With Psalm 1:1 in mind, note Genesis 13:

> So Lot chose for himself all the valley of the Jordan; and Lot journeyed eastward. Thus they separated from each other. [v. 11]

He *"walked in the way of the ungodly."*

> Abram settled in the land of Canaan, while Lot settled in the cities of the valley, and moved his tents as far as Sodom. Now the men of Sodom were wicked exceedingly and sinners against the Lord. [vv. 12–13]

He *"came and took his stand among sinners."*

And in Genesis 19:

Now the two angels came to Sodom in the evening as Lot was sitting in the gate of Sodom. . . . [v. 1]

He now lived among them with his dwelling in "the seat of the scornful."

How different was Joseph! He refused to allow the daily grind of compromise to take its toll even though Potiphar's wife continued to make her moves. Please stop and read Genesis 39:1–12. The man literally ran from her alluring advances. I find it most significant that every time sexual sins are mentioned in the New Testament we are told to "flee." Psalm 1:1 assures us we will be happy many times over if we check the first signals of compromise with evil. Happiness is maintaining unblemished, moral purity.

The song goes on: "But his delight is in the law of the Lord, / And in His law he meditates day and night (v. 2)."

This verse begins with *but*, a word of contrast. While the first verse was negative, this is positive. In contrast to compromise and erosion, the godly believer occupies himself with God's Word.

Why does David mention the Law here? Because in order to change our path of living, we need an absolute standard, clear direction. God's Word gives us that sense of direction. We understand the Law to be a reference to God's written Word, the Bible.

In Psalm 119:9, 11 we read:

> How can a young man keep his way pure?
> By keeping it according to Thy word. . . .
> Thy word I have treasured in my heart,
> That I may not sin against Thee.

The psalmist claims that the godly person "delights" in the Lord's Word. He doesn't look upon the Word as irksome or a burden or an interruption in his day. Rather, day and night he meditates on it. Even though he was busy and dedicated to the leadership of God's nation, Israel, David meditated on—placed his mind upon, mused, pondered, thought upon—the Scriptures day and night. He testifies to this in Psalm 119:97: "O how I love Thy law! / It is my meditation all the day."

Verse 1 of Psalm 1 gives us a promise of happiness; verse 2 provides the means for experiencing it. Now verse 3 declares the end result:

> And he will be like a tree firmly planted by streams of water,
> Which yields its fruit in its season,
> And its leaf does not wither;
> And in whatever he does, he prospers.

I am impressed that we shall *be* something rather than *do* something as a result of delighting in and meditating on God's Word. Without any fanfare, yet surely as the rising of the morning sun, we shall become treelike.

As I read the vivid lyrics of this verse, I discover four treelike characteristics of a godly life:

1. Planted—fortified, stable, rooted, solid, and strong
2. Fruitful—production naturally follows being planted and growing
3. Unwithered—even during days of difficulty, the treelike soul is undaunted
4. Prosperous—fulfills the goals God has designed for his life

I have said for years: "The roots grow deep when the winds are strong."

The prophet Jeremiah verifies this:

> Thus says the Lord,
> "Cursed is the man who trusts in mankind
> And makes flesh his strength,
> And whose heart turns away from the Lord.
> For he will be like a bush in the desert
> And will not see when prosperity comes,
> But will live in stony wastes in the wilderness,
> A land of salt without inhabitant.
> Blessed is the man who trusts in the Lord
> And whose trust is the Lord.

> For he will be like a tree planted by the water,
> That extends its roots by a stream
> And will not fear when the heat comes;
> But its leaves will be green,
> And it will not be anxious in a year of drought
> Nor cease to yield fruit." [Jer. 17:5–8]

Let me encourage you today to maintain a pure, uncompromising walk; delight yourself in His Word, and you'll grow into a stable, reliable "spiritual tree." There is no shortcut to spiritual growth. Like physical growth, it occurs on a daily basis, depending upon the food and proper surroundings.

With the right kind of spiritual diet and climate, *you can experience* "happiness many times over." And best of all, the daily grind of compromise and its erosive effects can be checked.

THE UNGODLY LIFE

A key observation in these verses is contrast. Don't miss the many things that are different from the preceding verses. "The wicked are not so, / But they are like chaff which the wind drives away."

"Not so!" That is exactly how verse 4 begins in the Hebrew Bible. It is an emphatic negative assertion. Literally, it says, "Not so, the wicked!"

It refers back to the three preceding verses describing the righteous, godly believer, who:

- is happy many times over (but "not so, the wicked!")
- delights and meditates in the Word (but "not so, the wicked!")
- is like a tree (but "not so, the wicked!")
- is fruitful and prosperous (but "not so, the wicked!")

In other words, none of the previously mentioned characteristics describes the lifestyle of the ungodly. Instead, the psalmist uses a single term that portrays the life of the ungodly—"chaff."

What is chaff? It is that outer part of the grain seeds which separates at the time of threshing—the husks and grasses which fall and blow about during harvest time. Chaff is completely worthless. It is the refuse and impurities blown away in the winnowing process. Chaff stands in contrast to the tree mentioned in verse 3. And to make this even more descriptive, look at the picturesque phrase which follows: ". . . like chaff which the wind drives away."

The Hebrew term translated "drives away" is the word which means "to drive asunder, disseminate, diffuse, strike, or beat." It is a harsh, buffeting picture.

Call to mind our Savior's words in Matthew 7:26–27:

And every one who hears these words of Mine, and does not act upon them, will be like a foolish man, who built his house upon the sand. And the rain descended, and the floods came, and the winds blew, and burst against that house; and it fell, and great was its fall.

Just as the winds and rains caused that house to fall because of an unstable foundation, so it will occur among the ungodly. Solomon's words provide a mental picture of the emptiness of life lived apart from fellowship with God:

And all that my eyes desired I did not refuse them. I did not withhold my heart from any pleasure, for my heart was pleased because of all my labor and this was my reward for all my labor. Thus I considered all my activities which my hands had done and the labor which I had exerted, and behold all was vanity and striving after wind and there was no profit under the sun. [Eccles. 2:10–11]

For what does a man get in all his labor and in his striving with which he labors under the sun? Because all his days his task is painful and grievous; even at night his mind does not rest. This too is vanity. [Eccles. 2:22–23]

Do you know the Lord Jesus Christ as your Savior? Are you building your life on His firm foundation? Or are you trying to construct order out of your inner chaos by the works of your own hands? Everything you produce this way falls in the category of "chaff."

Remember the warning in the First Psalm: "Therefore the wicked will not stand in the judgment, / Nor sinners in the assembly of the righteous" (v. 5).

The first word connects this verse with the previous verse—"Therefore [or on account of their inner worthlessness and instability] . . . the wicked will not stand in the judgment. . . ."

The Hebrew verb translated "stand" is not the same as the previous term rendered "stand" in verse 1. This particular Hebrew term means "to stand erect, to arise." The idea in the mind of the songwriter is an inability to stand erect before God's judgment. A parallel statement follows: ". . . Nor sinners in the assembly of the righteous."

The one who has never come by faith to the Lord and trusted Him alone for eternal life and a position of righteousness in God's eyes has no part among the assembly of believers. Again, let me remind you of yet another contrast. In destiny there is a great difference between the godly and the ungodly. But so many unbelievers live healthy, moral lives, even sacrificial and dedicated lives. How can anyone say they won't be among the eternal assembly of the righteous? Verse 6 answers that question: "For the Lord knows the way of the righteous, / But the way of the wicked will perish."

You'll observe it is *the Lord* who does the judging. He alone—not man—is capable of being just and fair. But doesn't the first part of this verse bring a question to your mind? Doesn't He know the way of the ungodly as well? He certainly does! But this sixth verse is explaining why the ungodly will not be able to stand up under judgment nor stand among the righteous assembly (v. 5). Why? Because the Lord takes special interest in the righteous. Because the Lord is inclined and bound to the righteous by special love, He will not allow an intermingling between the righteous and the unrighteous. That is not His plan.

The verse concludes with the severe reminder that the way of the unrighteous will perish. What a jolting climax to the psalm! Again, another vivid contrast. Instead of prospering, the ungodly will ultimately perish just as the little red brick city hall was ultimately condemned.

The central lesson in Psalm 1 is this: There is not the slightest similarity between the spiritually accelerating life of the righteous and the slowly eroding life of the wicked. Take time to ponder the bold contrasts:

Godly	Ungodly
Happiness many times over	Not so!
Uncompromised purity	Driven by the wind
Has a guide—Word of God	No guide mentioned
Like a tree	Like chaff
Stands erect before God	Unable to stand erect
Special object of God's care	No right to stand among righteous assembly
Destiny secure, safe, prosperous	Perish

Let's bring this week's study of Psalm 1 to a close with an expanded paraphrase:

Oh, the happiness, many times over, of the man who does not temporarily or even casually imitate the plan of life of those living in the activity of sinful confusion, nor comes and takes his stand in the midst of those who miss the mark spiritually, nor settles down and dwells in the habitation of the blasphemous crowd. But (in contrast to that kind of lifestyle) in God's Word he takes great pleasure, thinking upon it and pondering it every waking moment, day or night. The result: He will become treelike-firm, fruitful, unwithered, and fulfilling the goals in life that God has designed for him.

Not so, the ungodly! They are like worthless husks beaten about and battered by the winds of life (drifting and roaming without purpose). Therefore—on account of their inner worthlessness without the Lord—the ungodly are not able to stand erect on the day of judgment, nor do they possess any right to be numbered among the assembly of those declared righteous by God, because the Lord is inclined toward and bound to His righteous ones by special love and care; but the way of the one without the Lord will lead only to eternal ruin.

REFLECTIONS
ON COMPROMISE

1. Pause several times during this week and give yourself time to think deeply. Ask yourself a few probing questions such as:

   - Are areas of my life showing signs of spiritual, ethical, or moral compromise?
   - Am I really "happy many times over"?
   - Does my life resemble the kind of tree described in Psalm 1?
   - Should I put an end to some things that are dragging me down?

2. Read Psalm 1 again, this time aloud. Pay close attention to the "walk . . . stand . . . sit . . ." picture in the first verse. Honestly now, have you begun to tolerate a few compromises you once rejected? What will it take to get that cleared up? Never doubt the dangers brought on by spiritual, ethical, or moral erosion. Ponder the analogies between a building whose foundation is weakened and a person whose convictions are compromised.

3. This week, spend a few minutes each day—perhaps not more than two or three—delighting in the Lord. Tell Him in prayer how much you love Him and appreciate Him. Spell out why. Thank Him for removing most of the "chaff" that once weighed you down. And while you're at it, don't hide your relief; you might even smile more this week!

PSALM

For the choir director; for flute accompaniment.
A Psalm of David.

Give ear to my words, O Lord,
Consider my groaning.
Heed the sound of my cry for
help, my King and my God,
For to Thee do I pray.
In the morning, O Lord, Thou wilt hear
my voice;
In the morning I will order my prayer to
Thee and eagerly watch.

For Thou art not a God who takes
pleasure in wickedness;
No evil dwells with Thee.
The boastful shall not stand before Thine
eyes;
Thou dost hate all who do iniquity.
Thou dost destroy those who speak
falsehood;
The Lord abhors the man of bloodshed
and deceit.
But as for me, by Thine abundant
lovingkindness I will enter Thy house,
At Thy holy temple I will bow in
reverence for Thee.

O Lord, lead me in Thy righteousness
    because of my foes;
Make Thy way straight before me.
There is nothing reliable in what they
    say;
Their inward part is destruction itself;
Their throat is an open grave;
They flatter with their tongue.
Hold them guilty, O God;
By their own devices let them fall!
In the multitude of their transgressions
    thrust them out,
For they are rebellious against Thee.

But let all who take refuge in Thee be
    glad,
Let them ever sing for joy;
And mayest Thou shelter them,
That those who love Thy name may exult
    in Thee.
For it is Thou who dost bless the
    righteous man, O Lord,
Thou dost surround him with favor as
    with a shield.   [5:1–12]

THE GRIND OF DISCOURAGEMENT

The Book of Psalms is the oldest hymnal known to man. This ancient hymnal contains some of the most moving and meaningful expressions of the human heart.

Songs are usually born out of surrounding circumstances that so affect the thinking of the composer, he cannot help but burst forth with a melody and an accompanying set of lyrics describing his plight. This is certainly the case with the blues and jazz of yesteryear as well as the old spirituals of days gone by and the romantic love songs of any era. The same has often been true of gospel songs and sacred hymns; their historical settings explain their message.

Psalm 5 is no exception. As we read it, we can detect that it emerged out of an atmosphere of strife and oppression. David is down in the dumps . . . discouraged. Whatever his pressures were, they prompted him to compose an ancient hymn in the minor key.

I seriously doubt that there is any subject more timely than discouragement. So many folks I meet are playing out their entire lives in a minor key. There is the grinding discouragement that follows an unachieved goal or a failed romance. Some are discouraged over their marriage which began with such promise but now seems hopeless. Lingering ill-health can discourage and demoralize its victim, especially when the pain won't go away. And who can't identify with the individual who gave it his best shot yet took it on the chin from a few self-appointed critics? The discouragement brought on by several back-to-back criticisms can scarcely be exaggerated. It could be that David was just picking himself up off the mat when another sharp-worded comment knocked him back to his knees . . . hence the birth of Psalm 5.

Many a discouraged soul has identified with this song down through the centuries. Frequently, the words just above the first verse (which comprise the *superscription*) set forth the historical backdrop of the song.

If you glance just above verse 1 in the King James Version of the Bible, you will see that David desired this song to be played "upon Nehiloth." A nehiloth was an ancient woodwind instrument, something like today's flute or oboe. An oboe is a double-reed instrument giving a sad-sounding whine as it is being played. Its penetrating tone causes it to be used frequently as a solo instrument.

Interestingly, David did not play the nehiloth, but rather an ancient stringed instrument called the harp (see 1 Samuel 16:23, KJV). My point is simply this: David wrote this sad song of discouragement for someone else to play—not himself. Perhaps the surrounding circumstances were too overwhelming for him to participate in the playing of this piece. It could be rendered better by one who was skilled on the nehiloth. The sad tone of that instrument would enhance the feeling of discouragement which gave birth to this song.

OUTLINE

Some psalms are difficult to outline; others easily lend themselves to an organized layout. Psalm 5 falls in the latter category. It begins with a *plea* (vv. 1–3) directed to the Lord, whom David addresses, "O Lord . . . my King . . . my God . . . O Lord." It concludes with a *promise* (v. 12).

Sandwiched between the plea and the promise are four descriptions. An outline would look something like this:

    I. A Plea (vv. 1–3)
   II. Four Descriptions (vv. 4–11)
      A. What the Lord is like (vv. 4–6)

B. What the psalmist is like (vv. 7–8)
C. What the enemies are like (vv. 9–10)
D. What the righteous are like (v. 11)
III. A Promise (v. 12)

Take a look at David's introductory plea:

Give ear to my words, O Lord,
Consider my groaning.
Heed the sound of my cry for help, my King and my God,
For to Thee do I pray.
In the morning, O Lord, Thou wilt hear my voice;
In the morning I will order my prayer to Thee and eagerly
    watch. [vv. 1–3]

I observe three things in this plea.

First, it was a "morning" prayer. Twice in verse 3 David mentions that it was "in the morning" that he met with his Lord.

Second, it came from one who was becoming increasingly more discouraged. Look at the first two verses and notice how they grow in intensity: "Give ear to my words . . . consider my groaning . . . heed my cry!"

Hebrew poetry can be a complicated study, but some things about it are easy to grasp. One rather simple yet meaningful technique used in these two verses is what we might call synonymous parallelism. As the line progresses, the thoughts (though similar) increase in intensity. If this were played by an orchestra, there would perhaps be a crescendo sign appearing in the score. David is pleading: "Give ear!" Next, he becomes more burdened: "Consider!" He then grows stronger in his plea with the request that the Lord: "Heed the sound of my cry for help!" To enter into the depth of this hymn, you cannot afford to miss the growing discouragement in the writer's heart. Let yourself imagine his inner groaning. Picture the misery as you mentally relive his situation.

The third thing I observe in the psalmist's plea is that he anticipated God's intervention. By faith, he counted on it. I see two statements in verse 3 that reveal this: (1) "I will order my prayer to Thee" and (2) "I will eagerly watch."

The Hebrew verb translated *order* means "to make an order." The statement could read, "In the morning I will make my order to Thee." It is almost as if the composer had a menu in his hands. David looked upon the morning as the time to "place his order" with the Lord.

He then said, "I will eagerly watch" (literally, "look forward"). After placing his order, he eagerly anticipated an answer from his Lord.

David refused to stumble about stoop-shouldered, carrying his burdens throughout the day. On the contrary, he took his needs to the Lord each morning. When we think of "placing an order," we remember one thing that is essential: We have to be specific. Are you specific when you place your morning order? If there is one thing that plagues our prayer meetings and personal prayers it is vagueness. Could it be our generalities that keep us from witnessing direct and specific answers?

After David placed a specific order each morning, he anticipated answers. He expected God to "fill his order" and looked forward to that throughout the day. When our outlook is dim in the morning, when discouragement worms its way in, a good remedy is to focus our attention upward. And what a difference it makes in our day!

Frequently, the morning times are mentioned in Scripture as being especially meaningful to our spiritual lives. Let's review several examples:

For His anger is but for a moment,
His favor is for a lifetime;
Weeping may last for the night,
But a shout of joy comes in the morning. [Ps. 30:5]

Evening and morning and at noon, I will complain and murmur,
And He will hear my voice. [Ps. 55:17]

But I, O Lord, have cried out to Thee for help,
And in the morning my prayer comes before Thee. [Ps. 88:13]

The Lord's lovingkindnesses indeed never cease,
For His compassions never fail.
They are new every morning;
Great is Thy faithfulness. [Lam. 3:22–23]

And in the early morning, while it was still dark, He arose and went out and departed to a lonely place, and was praying there. [Mark 1:35]

After the plea in Psalm 5:1–3, David begins to think through the day that spreads out before him, and especially of those whom he would encounter. His song addresses four specific realms of interest (vv. 4–11). Let's look at each one of them:

1. David meditates on the Lord Himself (vv. 4–6).

> For Thou art not a God who takes pleasure in wickedness;
> No evil dwells with Thee.
> The boastful shall not stand before Thine eyes;
> Thou dost hate all who do iniquity.
> Thou dost destroy those who speak falsehood;
> The Lord abhors the man of bloodshed and deceit.

He mentions seven specific things about his Lord:

a. He takes no pleasure in wickedness.
b. No evil will "sojourn" with Him (literally).
c. Arrogant boasters will not stand before Him.
d. He hates workers of iniquity.
e. He destroys those who lie.
f. He abhors murderers.
g. He abhors deceivers.

Why does David review these things? Because it is a therapy to review the magnificent attributes of God. Many of the pent-up angry feelings and frustrations of our inner emotional tank are diffused as we spell out God's abilities. Focusing on His character helps dispel discouragement! Furthermore, we are reminded that *our* enemies are really *God's* enemies. And He is far more capable of dealing with them than we are.

2. David describes himself (vv. 7–8).

> But as for me, by Thine abundant lovingkindness I will
>   enter Thy house,
> At Thy holy temple I will bow in reverence for Thee.

♫

O Lord, lead me in Thy righteousness because of my foes;
Make Thy way straight before me.

Verse 7 begins with a strong contrast. The Hebrew is exceptionally strong, literally: "But me . . . as for me!"

In contrast to those whom the Lord would destroy (v. 6), David enjoyed a spiritual position, which is mentioned in the latter part of verse 7 as "Thy holy temple," a poetic reference to intimate fellowship with the Lord.

Verse 8 is the major prayer of this song. Everything before this verse could be considered preliminary. Here is the kernel of his request: "O Lord, lead me in Thy righteousness because of my foes; / Make Thy way straight before me."

What does this mean? David didn't want to resort to the tactics of his enemies, so he prayed that the Lord would lead him *His way* throughout the conflict. He wanted God's righteous way first and foremost. Not too many years later, the princely prophet Isaiah wrote similar words:

> "For My thoughts are not your thoughts,
> Neither are your ways My ways," declares the Lord.
> "For as the heavens are higher than the earth,
> So are My ways higher than your ways,
> And My thoughts than your thoughts." [Isa. 55:8–9]

3. <u>David then describes his enemies</u> (Ps. 5:9–10).

> There is nothing reliable in what they say;
> Their inward part is destruction itself;
> Their throat is an open grave;
> They flatter with their tongue.
> Hold them guilty, O God;
> By their own devices let them fall!
> In the multitude of their transgressions thrust them out,
> For they are rebellious against Thee.

In his mind, David deliberately hands his enemies over to God, who could handle them with no problem. He also asks God to allow them to "fall by their own devices." A very significant lesson to learn, when dealing with those who oppose righteousness, is to realize that they are fighting God, not you . . . therefore He is to be relied upon for your defense. Furthermore, if left alone in their own counsel, they will fall by themselves! Do you need the reminder from Romans 12:17–19? It says it straight.

> Never pay back evil for evil to anyone. Respect what is right in the sight of all men. If possible, so far as it depends on you, be at peace with all men. Never take your own revenge, beloved, but leave room for the wrath of God, for it is written, "Vengeance is Mine, I will repay," says the Lord.

The daily grind of discouragement is lessened when we focus on the Lord's fighting our battles for us.

4. <u>Finally, he describes the righteous</u> (Ps. 5:11).

> But let all who take refuge in Thee be glad,
> Let them ever sing for joy;
> And mayest Thou shelter them,
> That those who love Thy name may exult in Thee.

The key thought through this verse is obvious; it is joy. How are you doing regarding your countenance—is it joyful? Do you really live above the pressures? Is there an evidence of peace written across your face? If you fight your own battles without the Lord, you'll become bitter, severe, cranky, and your face will bear the marks of the battle.

Have you ever taken note of Cain's response to God's refusal of his offering? A most significant statement appears in Genesis 4:5: "So Cain became very angry and his countenance fell." Another way of translating the Hebrew text adds a bit more color: "And Cain burned with anger exceedingly and his face fell."

When anger and resentment are harbored, our faces show it. Our lips droop. Our eyes become sad. It is impossible to hide inner discouragement! "Fallen" faces are telltale signs of discouraged hearts. David wanted God to take his inner burden and replace it with inner joy.

Finally, the composer mentions in Psalm 5:12 a promise we frequently forget: "For it is Thou who dost bless the righteous man, O Lord, / Thou dost surround him with favor as with a shield."

David closes his song occupied with the Lord, having given Him his "morning burden." His discouragement has fled away. The shield he mentions at the end of his song here in verse 12 was the largest of warriors' shields, covering the entire body. So what is the promise? God will bless the one who looks to Him for protection. How? He will do this by giving him favor and by providing him with His large, protective (yet invisible) shield.

Up with the shield . . . out with discouragement!

EFLECTIONS ON DISCOURAGEMENT

1. Each morning of this week squeeze in some time to meet alone with the Lord. Just you and Him. If you are discouraged, admit it. Spell it out in detail. Take time to express the depth of your pain. Don't deny the reality of your sorrow. State your honest feelings. God can handle it!

2. While there, alone with the Lord, follow the guidelines of Psalm 5. Do you remember them?

   - Place your order. Be specific.
   - Review His attributes.
   - Tell Him how deeply you hurt. Describe why your face has "fallen" lately.
   - Remind yourself of His defense.
   - Call to mind two or three of His promises.
   - Stand firm on the Rock with a joyful countenance.

3. At least twice this week, tell someone why you are grateful to be alive . . . why you are more encouraged than you used to be. It will not only be therapy for you, it will lift that person's spirits as well. Wonderful changes can occur in us and others when we spread a few cheer germs around.

PSALM

For the choir director; on the Gittith.
A Psalm of David.

O Lord, our Lord,
How majestic is Thy name in
all the earth,
Who hast displayed Thy
splendor above the heavens!
From the mouth of infants and nursing
babes Thou hast established strength,
Because of Thine adversaries,
To make the enemy and the revengeful
cease.

When I consider Thy heavens, the work
of Thy fingers,
The moon and the stars, which Thou hast
ordained;
What is man, that Thou dost take thought
of him?
And the son of man, that Thou dost care
for him?

Yet Thou hast made him a little lower
than God,
And dost crown him with glory and
majesty!
Thou dost make him to rule over the
works of Thy hands;
Thou hast put all things under his feet,
All sheep and oxen,
And also the beasts of the field,
The birds of the heavens, and the fish of
the sea,
Whatever passes through the paths of the
seas.

O Lord, our Lord,
How majestic is Thy name in all the
earth!   [8:1–9]

THE GRIND OF FEELING OVERLOOKED

All of us need to be needed. It is satisfying to know that we can make a contribution or assist others in their need. Being in the swirl of activity, resourceful and responsive, we tend to think it'll never end. But it does. Sometimes ever so slowly through a chain of events or sometimes abruptly without warning, we find ourselves sidelined and no longer in demand. A tiny blood clot in the brain can seize our usefulness and leave us in its devastating wake. Another factor is age . . . merely growing older can move us away from the fast lane. By being passed over for a promotion or by being benched because a stronger player joins the team, we feel overlooked. It hurts.

The eighth song in God's ancient hymnal is a great one for those times in our lives when we feel bypassed, set aside, overlooked. It highlights the value God places upon His creatures, especially mankind.

There are three introductory observations that leap off the page as I read through the Eighth Psalm:

First, it is a psalm of David, written under the Holy Spirit's direction.

Second, it was designed to be "on the Gittith" (note the superscription, those words above verse 1). The etymology of this Hebrew term is questionable. Most probably *Gittith* is derived from Gath, an ancient Philistine city.

Do you remember David's most famous victory? Goliath, the

giant he slew, was from Gath (1 Sam. 17:4, 23). You, too, may have a giant to slay—that personal giant of feeling insignificant. So take heart; this song is for you.

The Scriptures also tell us that after David's victory over Goliath the people of Israel sang and danced as they celebrated the triumph (1 Sam. 18:6–7). I suggest—and it is only a suggestion—that this psalm was composed by David as a hymn of praise in honor of God who gave David that epochal triumph over Goliath of Gath. As you read the Eighth Psalm, you'll see that it seems to fit that historical backdrop.

My third observation is that Psalm 8 begins and ends with identical statements: "O Lord, our Lord, / How majestic is Thy name in all the earth. . . . " I find several interesting things about this repeated statement:

1. The psalmist speaks on behalf of the people of God, not just himself, hence *our* instead of *my*. This tells us he represents the people as he composes this song of victory.

2. The name of Jehovah is identified with *majestic*. This is from the Hebrew word *ah-daar*, meaning "wide, great, high, noble." David pictures our Lord as One who is gloriously magnificent, absolutely majestic!

3. The Lord's works and attributes are not limited to Israel or to the Land of Canaan. They are universal in scope. The Lord God is no national or tribal deity secluded from all else.

OUTLINE

Since seven and a half verses of Psalm 8 fall between repetitions of the same statement, we should understand that the twice-repeated statement is the central theme of the psalm. David worships the living Lord as the majestic and glorious Lord of all. Perhaps an outline of the song could resemble a public worship service all of us have attended:

   I. Doxology (v. 1a)
  II. Worship (vv. 1b–8)

   A. Praise (vv. 1b–2)
   B. Message (vv. 3–8)
      1. Man's Insignificance: "What is man?"
      2. God's Grace: "Thou . . . hast crowned him."
III. Benediction (v. 9)

DOXOLOGY

"O Lord, our Lord,
How majestic is Thy name in all the earth. . . . " [v. 1]

This first section declares the transcendent majesty and glory of God. Such a thought sets the tone of the psalm.

WORSHIP

As though standing before a congregation of believers, the songwriter reflects upon God's greatness and, in doing so, offers praise.

Praise

Who hast displayed Thy splendor above the heavens!
From the mouth of infants and nursing babes Thou hast
   established strength,
Because of Thine adversaries,
To make the enemy and the revengeful cease. [vv. 1–2]

The difference between praise and petition is the absence of self. David leaves himself out of the picture in this expression of praise. He declares that the majesty and glory of God are "displayed" in the heavens. The Lord has invested the physical universe with an awesome splendor of His majesty. Psalm 19:1 verifies this fact: "The heavens are telling of the glory of God; / And their expanse is declaring the work of His hands." And, again, Romans 1:20:

For since the creation of the world His invisible attributes, His eternal power and divine nature, have been clearly seen, being understood through what has been made.

David then goes on to illustrate his concept of God's glory by the other extreme—babes and infants. As tiny babies—even those still nursing—gurgle and smile, God shows Himself majestic and glorious.

I have an obstetrician friend who testifies that even before he became a Christian he could not ignore the power of God as he delivered and then held in his hands one tiny, screaming infant after another. He testifies that this ultimately led him to search for answers in the Bible and finally to find salvation through faith in Jesus Christ. In a very real sense, therefore, "infants and nursing babes" declare God's power and majesty. When we hear an infant's prattle, we have living proof of God's creative might. When we study the delicate little features of their new-born state, we marvel at His attention to detail. Verse 2 concludes with the reminder that even God's enemies are silenced when the heavens are observed . . . or when little ones are considered. Neither could reflect man's doing.

Infants may be small and the stellar spaces silent, but both convey a profound significance to the observer. So it is at those times in our lives when we may think we are no longer that valuable, that necessary. As long as we are alive, God can use us. There is an overwhelming comfort in the message that follows—the Creator loves His creation . . . He cares about us . . . we are special to Him.

Message

As though he were leading a worship service, David opens his mouth and shares a message from God, which is the major theme of his composition. We can imagine his standing before the people and preaching about man and God's grace.

1. Man's Insignificance.

"What is man?" Read verses 3–4 slowly. Think them over and enter into the mental picture David has in mind.

> When I consider Thy heavens, the work of Thy fingers,
> The moon and the stars, which Thou hast ordained,
> What is man that Thou dost take thought of him?
> And the son of man, that Thou dost care for him?

Let me call several things to your attention:

• The Hebrew word translated "consider" is the common verb meaning "to see, behold, take a look." David was out among the splendor of natural phenomena. As he looked about him he was gripped with the startling realization of God's greatness. Every one of us has had that experience. When we glance heavenward, we are struck with awe. We "take a look" at the expanse and, invariably, we are overwhelmed!

• David refers to God's creation as "the work of Thy fingers." Creation was merely the "fingerwork" of God, while salvation was His "armwork" (Isa. 52:10; 53:1; 59:16; Ps. 77:15, KJV).

• Based on his use of the words *the moon and the stars,*" I think we can conclude that it was at night when he wrote the psalm. Some of our best times for meditation present themselves in the night hours.

• In asking the question, "what is man?" David uses a rather uncommon term for man—*enosh,* from the Hebrew verb which means "to be weak, sick, frail." In other words: "In comparison to your splendor and majesty, O Lord—what is puny, weak, frail humanity?"

• God is said to perform two specific acts toward frail mankind:

  (a) Thou dost take thought of him.
  (b) Thou dost take care of him.

What do these things mean? The first statement means that God remembers us, while the second phrase means He pays attention to us. What an amazing thing! If the daily grind of feeling overlooked has you in its grip, here is a thought worth massaging. The God who created all the magnificent surroundings of the universe actually remembers and pays attention to puny individuals like you and me. It is easy to believe that God has too many other things to concern Himself with than to care about us. Peter reminds us, however, that "[God] cares for you" (1 Pet. 5:7). God never overlooks His own!

2. God's Grace.

> Yet Thou hast made him a little lower than God,
> And dost crown him with glory and majesty!
> Thou dost make him to rule over the works of Thy hands;
> Thou hast put all things under his feet,
> All sheep and oxen,
> And also the beasts of the field,
> The birds of the heavens, and the fish of the sea,
> Whatever passes through the paths of the seas. [Ps. 8:5–8]

In spite of the vast difference between God and man, David declares that the Lord has set His love upon us and has given humanity a place of dignity and importance in this world:

- We are made lesser than angels.
- We are nevertheless crowned with glory and majesty.
- We were made to rule over other earthly creatures (Gen. 1:28–30).

Hebrews 2:6–9 applies these verses to Jesus Christ, making this section of Psalm 8 messianic and prophetic. Historically, however, it is applicable to all humans. These three things are true of us.

When we stop and consider the impact of these verses, we quickly become humbled. Just to think that the Sovereign, Creator-God of the vast universe takes personal care of me is more than I can fathom. We who have large families sometimes find it difficult to stay current on all our little ones. (I embarrassingly confess I have even found it difficult to remember all their names in a hurried moment.) But never with God! He takes a personal interest in each one who trusts in Him. He adds oil to our grind of feeling overlooked by reminding us of His personal interest.

Perhaps as you read this you feel alone, deserted. What a distressing, barren valley is loneliness! But listen! If you have the Lord Jesus Christ as your personal Savior, you have a constant Companion and Friend. He never leaves you in the lurch. This psalm is proof positive that He does not consider you as unimportant or overlooked. He isn't irritated by our coming to Him with our needs. He never looks upon your prayers or requests as interruptions. Even as James reminds us: He gives "generously and without reproach" (1:5). He provides good gifts without "variation or shifting shadow" (1:17).

Do you know why? The answer is <u>Grace</u>—sheer, undeserved, unmerited, unearned favor. Therefore, right now cast your feeling of insignificance and despair on Him. Tell Him that you are claiming this Eighth Psalm as a promise of His personal grace, concern, and love for you.

Remember, this is a psalm "on the Gittith." David composed it perhaps as a victory hymn after defeating the giant Goliath. I challenge you to take that personal "giant" of feeling overlooked and ask God to give you victory over it today. Who knows? Another Goliath could fall by sundown.

BENEDICTION

David ends his song as he began it: "O Lord, our Lord, / How majestic is Thy name in all the earth" (v. 9). We add to David's benediction our own affirming response: Amen.

EFLECTIONS ON FEELING OVERLOOKED

1. This week, commit to memory the repeated phrase at the beginning and ending of the Eighth Psalm: "O Lord, our Lord, / How majestic is Thy name in all the earth."

2. Take the time late one night this week to walk out under the stars and look up. As you study the vast stellar spaces, give God praise for His wondrous works in the universe. Though silent, they reflect our God's majesty. You might be inclined to sing that great chorus of worship, "O Lord, our Lord, / How majestic is Thy name in all the earth." Be my guest!

3. Toward the end of the week, call to mind several recent occasions when He came to your rescue or gave you assistance or perhaps answered your prayer(s). Pause and thank Him because He cares for you. Tell Him how grateful you are for His attention to detail in every area of your life. Remind yourself of two or three specifics. The next time you are tempted to feel overlooked or passed by, remind yourself of His numerous kindnesses.

PSALM

For the choir director.
A Psalm of David.

How long, O Lord? Wilt Thou
  forget me forever?
How long wilt Thou hide Thy
  face from me?
How long shall I take counsel in my soul,
Having sorrow in my heart all the day?
How long will my enemy be exalted over
  me?

Consider and answer me, O Lord, my
  God;
Enlighten my eyes, lest I sleep the sleep
  of death,
Lest my enemy say, "I have overcome
  him,"
Lest my adversaries rejoice when I am
  shaken.

But I have trusted in Thy lovingkindness;
My heart shall rejoice in Thy salvation.
I will sing to the Lord,
Because He has dealt bountifully with
  me.   [13:1–6]

THE GRIND OF DESPONDENCY

Many years ago when I was living in Dallas, I received a phone call which led me to a tiny and dirty garage apartment. I was met at the screen door by a man with a 12-gauge shotgun. He invited me in. We sat for over an hour at a tiny kitchen table with a naked light bulb hanging above it. He poured out a heart-breaking story. He had just been released from the hospital, re-covering from back surgery. He was alone, having lost contact with his wife (and their only son) when his marriage failed many years before. As we talked of the man's intense struggles, I noticed that his small apartment was full of pictures—all of them of his son at various stages of growth.

There were photos taken of the boy when he was still in diapers. Others were with his dad when the lad was graduating from kindergarten. Still others showed him in his Little-League uniform with a bat over his shoulder . . . on and on, right up through high school. The man's entire focus centered upon a marriage that had failed and especially a boy he no longer was able to enjoy. Those nostalgic "misty, water-colored memories of the way we were" held him captive in a prison-house of despondency. Unfortunately, my attempts to help him see beyond the walls of his anguish proved futile. In less than a week, he shot himself to death in his car which he had driven deep into the woods in East Texas. To him, life was no longer worth the fight.

It is not necessary to read Psalm 13 many times to detect a despondency in David. Like my lonely friend in the apartment, the psalmist feels down. Forgotten. It is that age-old "nobody seems to care" syndrome. Despair may not be too strong a description of his emotional temperature. Obviously, he is "under the pile." We understand! I'm convinced it is these mutual feelings that cause us to be drawn to the Psalms on our blue days. David feels miserable. We wonder why. No one can say for sure, for the background of many of the psalms remains a mystery.

We do know, however, that some of David's darkest days came before he was officially promoted to the throne of Israel. God was preparing him for an immense task, and He used the trials to shape him into a man of maturity and inner strength. It may help us to look back into 1 Samuel for what might have been the circumstances which led David to write this song. (See 1 Sam. 18:9–15, 28–29; 20:30–33.)

He had just slain Goliath of Gath. The Philistines, therefore, had become a defeated foe of Israel and David had become the most famous (though still youthful) hero in the land. As a result, the people sang his praises which, in the process, aroused King Saul's jealousy. How he hated David's popularity! As a result, Saul fell into such a fit of hostility he became dead set on murdering David. Exit: harmony. Enter: despondency.

Think of it! From that time on, David became the object of Saul's diabolical plan. Though innocent before God and loyal to King Saul, David literally ran for his life and lived as an escaped fugitive in the hills of Judea for over a dozen years.

Hunted and haunted by madman Saul, David must have entertained doubts at times. He often had no one but the Lord to turn to in his despondent moments. There he was, the anointed king-elect, existing like a beast in the wilderness, running for his life. (That would disillusion anyone!) I can imagine David slumped beside several large bushes or hidden beneath a boulder alongside some mountain—dirty and despondent, wondering if the chase would ever end.

With that as a backdrop, Psalm 13 makes a lot of sense.

OUTLINE

This psalm, as so many, is a prayer directed to Jehovah. It includes six verses that build toward a climax. It begins in the pit of despondency and concludes on the mountain peaks of ecstasy.

   I. David is down, flat *on his face*—focused on his misery and complaints (vv. 1–2).
     A. He focuses on the depth of the trial.
     B. He focuses on the length of the trial.
  II. David is *on his knees*—taking his burden to the Lord and admitting his own dependence upon Him (vv. 3–4).
 III. David is *on his feet*, rejoicing and singing (vv. 5–6).

DAVID ON HIS FACE

> How long, O Lord? Wilt Thou forget me forever?
> How long wilt Thou hide Thy face from me?
> How long shall I take counsel in my soul,
> Having sorrow in my heart all the day?
> How long will my enemy be exalted over me? [vv. 1–2]

Swamped by the overwhelming trials of life, David resorts to four common and human ways to handle despondency. In these two verses he reminds us of ourselves and four mental escape routes we often take under pressure.

1. God has forgotten me—forever. (Remember the last time you felt that abandoned?) "How long, O Lord? Wilt Thou forget me forever?"

Since the testing had continued so long without hope of relief, David finally became emotionally crushed beneath the load and wondered if God had abandoned him.

2. God doesn't care about me. (Gross self-pity.) "How long wilt Thou hide Thy face from me?"

This inevitably accompanies feelings of abandonment. God has simply lost interest. He said He would take care of me and bear my burdens and lift my load, but that isn't the case! (Sound a little familiar?) God's Word is so very practical. How often we see ourselves reflected on the pages of the Bible.

3. I'm going to have to work things out for myself. (No faith in God's promises.) "How long shall I take counsel in my soul? . . ."

The Hebrew term translated *take counsel* means to "plan." David had begun to plan a way out, adjust matters himself. "After all," he might have said, "God gave me a mind and He expects me to use it. God helps those who help themselves!"

Hold it! Is that true? That statement never appears in Scripture! Let's pause and remind ourselves of several of Solomon's sayings:

> Trust in the Lord with all your heart,
> And do not lean on your own understanding.
> In all your ways acknowledge Him,
> And He will make your paths straight. [Prov. 3:5–6]

> Commit your works to the Lord,
> And your plans will be established. [Prov. 16:3]

> When a man's ways are pleasing to the Lord,
> He makes even his enemies to be at peace with him. [Prov. 16:7]

> The lot is cast into the lap,
> But its every decision is from the Lord. [Prov. 16:33]

What happens when we try to work things out in our own flesh? Exactly what happened to David. And what was that? Look at the next part of Psalm 13:2, "Having sorrow in my heart all the day."

Sorrow, strain, frustration, and worry became his constant companions. Such are the byproducts of do-it-yourself activities. WHEN WILL WE EVER LEARN TO LEAVE OUR BURDENS WITH THE LORD AND LET HIM WORK OUT THE DETAILS?

4. I resent this trial! It's humiliating to endure being stepped on. (Pride has now been wounded, so it retaliates.) "How long will my enemy be exalted over me?"

Isn't this a typical complaint? Again, I remind you, it comes from pride. It says, in effect, that I have the right to defend the truth, especially when it comes to some enemy taking advantage of me. How we fight to maintain our pride! How we long to be appreciated and well-thought-of! David was having to learn that the truth will defend itself. It will emerge as the champion in God's own time.

Immediately, I see two strategic areas of application:

1. "How long" occurs four times in two brief verses. It was the length of the test that began to weary David. Let us remember that God not only designs the depth of our trials but also their length. Sometime soon, read the words of the ancient prophet Habakkuk, chapter 1. He, too, asked, "How long?"

2. In the first two verses of Psalm 13 David turns against everyone and everything except himself. What I learn from this is that when I try to handle a test in the flesh, I turn against God, my enemy, or my circumstance rather than first asking the Lord what He is trying to teach me in this situation. What wonderful lessons God wishes to teach us if our proud hearts would only be willing to melt in the furnace of affliction.

DAVID ON HIS KNEES

Consider and answer me, O Lord, my God;
Enlighten my eyes, lest I sleep the sleep of death,
Lest my enemy say, "I have overcome him,"
Lest my adversaries rejoice when I am shaken. [vv. 3–4]

Something happened to David between stanzas 2 and 3 of his hymn. Perhaps he listened to his own complaints and realized it was self-pity. (I've done that, haven't you?) Maybe he paused in his composition and looked back over what he had just written . . . and became alarmed at the unbelief that began to surface before his eyes. We observe a genuine and marked difference now. He is up off his face. His despondency is beginning to lift. We find him, at last, on his knees—the place of victory. The martyred missionary, Jim Elliot, once wrote: "The saint who advances on his knees never retreats."

Please observe how closely verses 3 and 4 are connected with verses 1 and 2. David seems to recollect and redirect his complaints as he talks to the Lord about them. Three changes become apparent:

First, instead of viewing the Lord as being removed and un-concerned (v. 1), David requests that He "consider and answer" him (v. 3). And don't miss what he calls the Lord in verse 3— "my God!" The distance is now gone in David's mind. He is embracing an altogether different outlook.

Second, instead of the despondency and distress that had become his heart attitude due to his attempts to work things out (v. 2), he now asks the Lord to "enlighten my eyes."

Again, the Hebrew gives us a clearer understanding of this. The word translated *enlighten* in verse 3 is in the causative stem, meaning literally "to cause to shine." In Numbers 6:24–26 the identical term occurs in a benediction we've heard many times:

> The Lord bless you, and keep you;
> The Lord *make His face* shine on you,
> And be gracious to you;
> The Lord lift up His countenance on you,
> And give you peace. [Emphasis is mine.]

David's countenance had lost its "shine." His face, and espe-cially his eyes, had become hard, flat, and dull. He longed for God's brightness to reflect itself once again from his eyes—his face had fallen.

When trials are dealt with in the flesh, I want to state once again that the eyes bear the marks of that fact. We cannot hide it. Our entire countenance becomes rigid and inflexible, lacking the "sparkle" and the "light" that once manifested itself from our hearts. When inner joy leaves, so does the "shine" from our eyes.

Third, instead of worrying about his exalted enemy (v. 2), David now mentally releases his enemy to the Lord and lets Him take care of the results (v. 4).

I notice this marked change in David occurred when he decided to lay it all out before God in prayer. Although it sounds like a cliché, our fervent petition is still the most effective oil to reduce the friction from the daily grind of despondency. A portion of an old Christian hymn states:

> O what peace we often forfeit,
> O what needless pain we bear,
> All because we do not carry
> Ev'rything to God in prayer.[1]

Yes, *everything*.

DAVID ON HIS FEET

> But I have trusted in Thy lovingkindness;
> My heart shall rejoice in Thy salvation.
> I will sing to the Lord,
> Because He has dealt bountifully with me. [vv. 5–6]

The first word in verse 5 is *but*. That little word usually introduces a contrast to the reader. It's as if David were saying, "In contrast to my earlier complaints and fears, my dull eyes and proud heart. . . . I have trusted! . . . My heart shall rejoice! . . . I will sing!"

Notice his exclamations of praise? What a delightful difference! This sounds more like the David we know, doesn't it? We dare not overlook the last part of the final verse: "Because He has dealt bountifully with me."

How significant! Read it again, then stop and think. David's circumstances had not changed. Saul still hunted him. The barren slopes of Judea were still barren. His hunger, if present before he wrote the psalm, was still a reality. *Nothing around the man was different*, and yet David's conclusions were 180 degrees from his original thoughts. Why? Because *David* had changed. God had "dealt bountifully" with him.

APPLICATION

Trials are designed for *us*, not for our surroundings. God wishes to train us, to mold us. He uses the distressing circumstances of life as His tools. He allows the icy feelings of despondency to linger within us. In doing so, He deals bountifully with us . . . deep within where no one else can see or touch.

We have not learned the most basic and essential lessons God has designed for us in any given trial until we can say, "He has dealt bountifully with me."

In the magnificent Psalm 119, David declares this same conclusion in verses 71 and 75. In fact, he says such trials are *good* for us!

> It is good for me that I was afflicted,
> That I may learn Thy statutes. . . .
> I know, O Lord, that Thy judgments are righteous,
> And that in faithfulness Thou hast afflicted me.

This is what the apostle Paul came to realize from his "thorn in the flesh" as he wrote in 2 Corinthians 12:9–10 (KJV):

> And he said unto me, "My grace is sufficient for thee: for my strength is made perfect in weakness." Most gladly therefore will I rather glory in my infirmities, that the power of Christ may rest upon me. Therefore I take pleasure in infirmities, in reproaches, in necessities, in persecutions, in distresses for Christ's sake: for when I am weak, then I am strong.

Weakness is not a symptom of a terminal disease. It is simply tangible proof of our humanity. Better still, it is the platform upon which God does some of His most magnificent work.

If the daily grind of despondency has begun to wrap its clammy fingers around you and drag you under, let me encourage you to get better acquainted with this unique song of new hope. It can be not only a comfort to your soul . . . very likely it will lift you off your face and put you back on your feet.

REFLECTIONS ON DESPONDENCY

1. Has despondency begun to dog your steps? If so, it might be helpful to retrace your path and locate what prompted your discouraged feelings. Is your focus on "The way we were"? Do you have some Saul making your life miserable? Are you struggling with a subtle pressure that increases each day? Starting to feel abandoned and alone? Has something aroused your anger? Now is a good time to get on your knees (yes, literally on your knees) and unload your burden from your shoulders and into the Lord's lap—where it belongs. Don't worry, He can handle it!

2. Let's be painfully honest, okay? Take stock of how you have handled the stress in recent days. Have you attempted to work things out in the energy of the flesh? If so, say so. Have you been protecting your pride? Come on . . . admit it. In fact, go a step further and tell the Lord you are weary of fighting your own battles. Ask Him to step in, take charge, and be your defense.

3. As David concludes his song, he writes, "I will sing to the Lord. . . ." Do that. Choose a different hymn of praise each day this week and sing it aloud to the Lord. Without a song, remember, life gets pretty grim.

_P_SALM

A Psalm of David.

O Lord, who may abide in Thy
    tent?
    Who may dwell on Thy holy
      hill?
He who walks with integrity, and works
    righteousness,
And speaks truth in his heart.
He does not slander with his tongue,
Nor does evil to his neighbor,
Nor takes up a reproach against his
    friend;
In whose eyes a reprobate is despised,
But who honors those who fear the Lord;
He swears to his own hurt, and does not
    change;
He does not put out his money at
    interest,
Nor does he take a bribe against the
    innocent.
He who does these things will never be
    shaken. [15:1–5]

THE GRIND OF WEAKENED INTEGRITY

Benjamin Franklin once called this song the "Gentlemen's Psalm." To him, it represented the standard of life after which a gentleman should pattern his walk. As fine a description as that may be, David's song goes even deeper than that—it is indeed the "Christian's Psalm." It sets forth, not so much the way a person finds the Lord, as it does the way we are to live after the Lord has entered our life. In other words, it doesn't deal with how someone becomes a Christian, but rather how a Christian should maintain a life of integrity. It sets forth many of the moral and ethical characteristics God desires in His children's day-to-day lifestyle, both in public and in private.

It should come as a surprise to no one that ours is a day of weakened integrity. Pause for a moment and call to mind a few of the more prominent examples:

- U.S. Marines stationed at our embassy in Russia whose duty it was to protect confidential documents traded our secrets for sexual gratification.
- A couple of high-profile politicians who had begun their move toward the presidency were forced to pull out . . . one because of blatant acts of plagiarism, the other because of questionable morals.
- Our space program took a giant step backward as the Challenger exploded shortly after being launched, killing the entire crew. Critical-thinking engineers who had said no

during the countdown were outvoted by several bureau-
crats who ignored the warnings regarding a leaky seal.
- Even the religious world has not escaped a breakdown in
  integrity. Sex scandals and the misuse of ministry funds
  have put a black eye on the face of several televangelists,
  which cannot help but bruise the testimony of other media
  ministries even though they may be squeaky clean. When a
  cloud of suspicion appears over several well-knowns, even
  the obscure are affected by the shadow.

If your daily grind is a weakened integrity, this song will
speak volumes to you.

BACKGROUND

No one knows what prompted David to write this song. All
we know is that he did, in fact, write it. There is a broader
biblical background, however, that causes the psalm to take on
real significance. Let me explain.

The moment a believing sinner gives his heart to Jesus Christ,
he is declared to be the recipient of numerous spiritual blessings.
These make up our eternal inheritance, which never changes.
We become a child of God (John 1:12), adopted into His family
forever (Rom. 8:14–17), sealed and secure (Eph. 1:13), delivered
from darkness into God's love (Col. 1:13), a priest (1 Pet. 2:9),
and on and on! These things never change regardless of our
walk. They become our permanent inheritance. In that way, they
represent our unchanged eternal position in God's eyes.

But something else is also true—we have temporal fellowship with our Lord. From salvation onward, the child of God
has the privilege of living under the control of the Holy Spirit.
The flip side of that arrangement introduces a possibility: He
may choose to sin and walk under the energy of his own flesh
and thus break this temporal fellowship that is his to claim.
When he does, he chooses to reject God's power and blessing
and moves immediately out of the realm of fellowship into the
realm of divine discipline. Let me hasten to add that his tragic

loss of temporal fellowship need not be extended. If the believer will confess his sins (1 John 1:9) and begin to walk in dependence upon the Holy Spirit (Gal. 5:16; Eph. 5:18), temporal fellowship will immediately be restored.

How does all this tie in with Psalm 15? Simply that this divine song has to do with our walking in the realm of temporal fellowship. In fact, it mentions some of the things we should be doing within the framework of that fellowship. It deals with those works of righteousness which are prompted by the Holy Spirit while we are walking in dependence upon our God. When these things begin to fade from our lives, our integrity is inevitably weakened—ultimately, our testimony is hurt.

OUTLINE

If you read Psalm 15 carefully, you will discover that it all hangs upon the first verse. Verse 1 is crucial in that it asks a key question. Answering it becomes the object of the rest of the verses. The song then concludes with a wonderful promise. A simple outline could be:

I. Question: "Who may abide in Thy tent? . . . " (v. 1)
II. Answer: "He who walks with integrity . . . " (vv. 2–5)
III. Promise: "He will never be shaken" (v. 5)

THE QUESTION

O Lord, who may abide in Thy tent?
Who may dwell on Thy holy hill? [v. 1]

The song opens with a prayer directed to Jehovah. Two questions are asked with the same thought in mind. Literally, they read: "Jehovah, who shall dwell in your tent? Who shall settle down on your holy mountain?"

The references to God's "tent" and "holy mountain" are symbols of God's presence—descriptive expressions of intimate fellowship. In other words, David is asking, "What kind of an individual does it take to maintain and enjoy intimate fellowship with You, Lord?"

THE ANSWER

> He who walks with integrity, and works righteousness,
> And speaks truth in his heart.
> He does not slander with his tongue,
> Nor does evil to his neighbor,
> Nor takes up a reproach against his friend;
> In whose eyes a reprobate is despised,
> But who honors those who fear the Lord;
> He swears to his own hurt, and does not change;
> He does not put out his money at interest,
> Nor does he take a bribe against the innocent. [vv. 2–5]

Now David sets out to answer that key question. I count eleven specific characteristics, each of which is worth our attention this week.

1. He who walks with integrity. This has to do with *who we are* as well as *where we go*. The word *integrity* means "to be solid, wholesome, complete." The believer who is interested in maintaining temporal fellowship is careful about how he lives and where he goes—he walks in the realm of truth. He refuses to live a lie.

2. He who works righteousness. This has to do with *what we do*. Righteousness is to be the habit of our conscious life. Our dealings are to be honest, our activities clear of compromise. In today's vernacular, we're to "keep our nose clean." To do less is to weaken our integrity.

3. He who speaks truth in his heart. This has to do with *how we think.* Notice that the truth mentioned here is spoken "in the heart"—attitudes, reactions, and motives are in David's mind. The source of these things (the heart—Prov. 23:7, KJV) is to be a bedrock of truth, no place for deception or lies or a hidden agenda!

4. He who does not slander with his tongue. This and the next two characteristics have to do with *what we say.* The Hebrew word translated *slander* literally means "to go about, to foot it"—we might even say "to hoof it." It would include one who walks here and there spreading malicious slander, pouring out verbal venom and poisoning others behind their backs.

This is an excellent time for me to pose a direct question. Does this describe you? Are you a gossip? Do you inwardly enjoy hearing or passing on some juicy tale that colors another's reputation? It is interesting that in the list of seven things God hates (Prov. 6:16–19) three have to do with the tongue.

Several years ago I was given wise counsel regarding the use of my tongue. I hope it will help you as much as it has helped me:

Before you pass along information or comments about someone else, let it first pass through four gates for approval. If all four give you a green light, share it without hesitation:

Gate 1: Is it confidential? (If so, never mention it.)
Gate 2: Is it true? (This may take some investigation.)
Gate 3: Is it necessary? (So many words are useless.)
Gate 4: Is it kind? (Does it serve a wholesome purpose?)

Here's another good piece of advice: If you ever have to say, "I really shouldn't say this . . . ," *don't!* Few statements from Scripture are more pointed on this subject than Ephesians 4:29. Look at it as it is recorded in The Modern Language Bible, The Berkeley Version in Modern English:

Let no foul speech come out of your mouth, but only such as will build up where it is necessary, so as to add a blessing to the listeners.

5. He who does not do evil to his neighbor. The Spirit-filled believer is loyal and consistent—not fickle, not erratic. He does not consciously bring difficulty upon others.

6. Nor takes up a reproach against his friend. This means he does not say sharp, cutting, and scornful things about others,

either behind their back or to their face. There is honesty yet gentleness (Gal. 5:22–23) in his character.

7. In whose eyes a reprobate is despised. This has to do with *who we are with.* A reprobate mentioned here is literally a "worthless reprobate," someone who is totally disinterested in spiritual things. The genuine believer with strong integrity will discern the impact such a person can have on his own walk with the Lord, and will not cultivate an association with him. "Do not be deceived: 'Bad company corrupts good morals'" (1 Cor. 15:33).

8. He honors those who fear the Lord. Like the preceding phrase, this is still dealing with our associates, only this phrase is the other side of the coin. It addresses those with whom we *should* keep company. The believer who walks with the Lord has a scale of values that is determined by biblical principles. Since we become like those with whom we spend our time, a Christlike friend needs to be sought out for companionship.

9. He swears to his own hurt, and does not change. This means that we perform what we promise, even when keeping our word is difficult to achieve. Our word should be our bond. The Christian with integrity makes it his aim to do what he says he will do, even when it hurts—even when it is inconvenient.

10. He does not put out his money at interest. According to Deuteronomy 23:19–20 and Leviticus 25:35–38, the Jew was commanded not to loan a needy Jewish brother money on interest. He was to assist generously and unselfishly. The believer in Christ who offers to extend personal financial assistance to his brother in Christ should do so without interest, love being his only motive. (Needless to say, discernment must accompany love . . . or we will have more love than money!) Not every financial need among believers is a "need." Some "needs" stem from careless spending.

11. Nor does he take a bribe against the innocent. My Webster's dictionary defines a bribe as "money or favor bestowed on

or promised to a person in a position of trust to pervert his judgment or corrupt his conduct." We have all read about what has come to be known as "influence peddling." Not even Wall Street has been protected from such schemes. The psalmist's point is clear: One with integrity won't stoop to that level.

THE PROMISE

. . . he who does these things will never be shaken. [v. 5]

We are promised that if these things become our practice, we will live stable, solid, dependable lives. Those who bring these areas under the control of the Holy Spirit will live wholesome lives as solid citizens of heaven. Or, using Ben Franklin's suggestion, whoever lives like this will be considered a "Christian gentleman." Such people are rare, indeed. No wonder they are not easily shaken! Integrity reinforces a life with steel.

EFLECTIONS ON WEAKENED INTEGRITY

1. Get a dictionary, look up *integrity,* and write the definition below:

   _____

   _____

   _____

   Study that definition with an eye on applying it to your life. What stands out?

2. Spend this week reviewing the eleven marks of solid Christian integrity. Does one or two of them bring an extra pang of conviction? Go ahead and admit it. Ask the Lord to assist you this week as you think of ways to strengthen those weaknesses.

3. As the week passes, look for these eleven qualities of integrity in others. Whenever you witness them, thank the person for demonstrating such fine character. Let me add a further suggestion. When you hear or read of someone in the public arena who resisted the temptation to weaken his or her integrity, write that person and express your respect. Affirmation fuels the fire of strong character.

PSALM

For the choir director.
A Psalm of David.

The heavens are telling of the
glory of God;
And their expanse is declaring
the work of His hands.
Day to day pours forth speech,
And night to night reveals knowledge.
There is no speech, nor are there words;
Their voice is not heard.
Their line has gone out through all the
earth,
And their utterances to the end of the
world.
In them He has placed a tent for the sun,
Which is as a bridegroom coming out of
his chamber;
It rejoices as a strong man to run his
course.
Its rising is from one end of the heavens,
And its circuit to the other end of them;
And there is nothing hidden from its
heat.

The law of the Lord is perfect, restoring
the soul;
The testimony of the Lord is sure, making
wise the simple.
The precepts of the Lord are right,
rejoicing the heart;

The commandment of the Lord is pure,
enlightening the eyes.
The fear of the Lord is clean, enduring
forever;
The judgments of the Lord are true; they
are righteous altogether.
They are more desirable than gold, yes,
than much fine gold;
Sweeter also than honey and the
drippings of the honeycomb.
Moreover, by them Thy servant is
warned;
In keeping them there is great reward.
Who can discern his errors? Acquit me of
hidden faults.
Also keep back Thy servant from
presumptuous sins;
Let them not rule over me;
Then I shall be blameless,
And I shall be acquitted of great
transgression.
Let the words of my mouth and the
meditation of my heart
Be acceptable in Thy sight,
O Lord, my rock and my
redeemer.   [19:1–14]

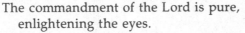

THE GRIND OF DIVINE SILENCE

Ever felt totally removed from God's awareness? It's almost like you are standing at the bottom of a long stairway looking up. The light is off, and even though you knock or call out for a response, nothing happens. There isn't even a stir.

You are not alone. Many a soul struggles at this very moment with divine silence. And to make matters worse, it grinds on for days, sometimes weeks. Following a calamity, the victim crawls out, cries out, and expects overnight relief. It doesn't come. A mate who has been there for years suddenly packs it in and walks out. The one who is left alone to face what seems to be endless responsibilities turns to God for His intervention—for His comforting reassurance only to be met with silence. That awful silence! Equally difficult is a lingering illness. No prayer, it seems, is effective. As the deafening silence continues from above, pain intensifies below.

Believe it or not, this grand song that directs our attention to the skies has something to say about those anguishing times of silence on earth. In beautiful ways the heavens above us speak with profound wisdom.

The philosopher Kant once wrote:

> There are two things that fill my soul with holy reverence and evergrowing wonder—the spectacle of the starry sky that virtually annihilates us as physical beings, and the moral law which raises us to infinite dignity as intelligent agents.[2]

Kant could have been influenced by the Nineteenth Psalm when he wrote that statement, for this song describes both of the things that filled his soul with reverence and wonder.

If you read the lyrics carefully, you will discover that they fall naturally into two sections. So obvious is the dividing line that some have come to the conclusion it was composed by two different people—each emphasizing a particular subject. Such is not the case, however, for David is named as the single writer.

OUTLINE

The dividing line falls between verses 6 and 7. The first section (vv. 1–6) deals with the world God has created. It describes in vivid fashion the fact that His creative work sets forth His power and His glory. The second section (vv. 7–13) deals with the truth God has communicated. It describes some of the benefits derived from the Scriptures as well as the discernment it can bring to one's personal life. The song concludes with a prayer (v. 14). What a message of hope it brings to all who struggle with the grind of divine silence. All the way through the song, David reminds us that the Lord is not only close to His creatures, He cares for us as well.

 I. The World God Has Created (vv. 1–6)
  A. Overall Declaration (vv. 1–4)
   1. Consistent (vv. 1–2)
   2. Silent (v. 3)
   3. Universal (v. 4)
  B. Specific Illustration—the Sun (vv. 4–6)
   1. Appearance Described (vv. 4–5)
    a. "tent"
    b. "bridegroom"
    c. "strong man"
   2. Activity Described (v. 6)
    a. "its rising"
    b. "its circuit"
    c. "its heat"

   II. The Truth God Has Communicated (vv. 7–13)
      A. Its Presence among Us (vv. 7–9)
          1. Titles (five are given)
          2. Characteristics (six are given)
          3. Benefits (four are given)
      B. Its Value to Us (v. 10)
          1. Gold . . . fine gold
          2. Honey . . . honeycomb
      C. Its Work within Us (vv. 11–13)
          1. Warning
          2. Rewarding
          3. Discerning
          4. Revealing
  III. Closing prayer (v. 14)

We will hit only the highlights of these fourteen verses because neither time nor space permits us to dig into the depths of each one. However, I urge you to take the outline and use it as a guide in your own, personal study of this magnificent composition. It is a veritable treasure house of truth.

THE WORLD GOD HAS CREATED

> The heavens are telling of the glory of God;
> And their expanse is declaring the work of His hands.
> Day to day pours forth speech,
> And night to night reveals knowledge.
> There is no speech, nor are there words;
> Their voice is not heard.
> Their line has gone out through all the earth,
> And their utterances to the end of the world.
> In them He has placed a tent for the sun,
> Which is as a bridegroom coming out of his chamber;
> It rejoices as a strong man to run his course.
> Its rising is from one end of the heavens,
> And its circuit to the other end of them;
> And there is nothing hidden from its heat. [vv. 1–6]

For six verses David looks heavenward. He ponders the vast spaces beyond, that realm we call natural phenomena. He tells us that God uses "the heavens" and "their expanse" to declare His glory and His power (v. 1).

After this general statement, David reminds us that this declaration is (1) consistent—"day to day . . . night to night," (2) silent—"no speech, nor . . . words . . . Their voice is not heard," and (3) universal—"all the earth . . . to the end of the world."

God's majestic universe contains a message. It is, in fact, a bold announcement! Regardless of the time of day, location, or our native language, if we look up, we are able to "hear" His message! And what, specifically, is the message? The answer is in Romans 1:18–20:

> For the wrath of God is revealed from heaven against all ungodliness and unrighteousness of men, who suppress the truth in unrighteousness, because that which is known about God is evident within them; for God made it evident to them. For since the creation of the world His invisible attributes, His eternal power and divine nature, have been clearly seen, being understood through what has been made, so that they are without excuse.

Did you grasp that? God reveals "His eternal power and divine nature" so clearly that everyone is left "without excuse." Don't tell me that God has hidden Himself from the world! Every intelligent being lives every waking moment under the constant reminder of God's presence, sovereignty, and power. Stubborn unbelief causes humanity to miss God's persistent message. Anyone who struggles with the mystery of divine silence—whether it's while picking up the pieces after a disaster, or recovering from the loss of a loved one, or trying to find a burst of hope to go on beyond a divorce—needs only to look up. God is speaking!

More specifically, consider the sun's symbolism in Psalm 19:4–6: Both its appearance and activity provide ample information to anyone who asks: "Is there a God?" No one other than our God could create, sustain, and employ such a heavenly body as the sun. Its size, temperature, and distance from us (thanks to the perfect filter system of our atmosphere) provide us with just the right level of heat and light.

THE TRUTH GOD HAS COMMUNICATED

The law of the Lord is perfect, restoring the soul;
The testimony of the Lord is sure, making wise the simple.
The precepts of the Lord are right, rejoicing the heart;
The commandment of the Lord is pure, enlightening the eyes.
The fear of the Lord is clean, enduring forever;
The judgments of the Lord are true; they are righteous
    altogether.
They are more desirable than gold, yes, than much fine gold;
Sweeter also than honey and the drippings of the honeycomb.
Moreover, by them Thy servant is warned;
In keeping them there is great reward.
Who can discern his errors? Acquit me of hidden faults.
Also keep back Thy servant from presumptuous sins;
Let them not rule over me;
Then I shall be blameless,
And I shall be acquitted of great transgression.
Let the words of my mouth and the meditation of my heart
Be acceptable in Thy sight,
O Lord, my rock and my redeemer. [vv. 7–13]

The heavens may declare God's power and glory, but they do not declare His will or His plan and promise of salvation. God has communicated those marvelous truths in His Word—the living Scriptures, the Bible. Notice the change from God (vv. 1–6) to Lord (vv. 7–14). David includes in this second part of the song a more personal example of *God's presence.*

Observe first the <u>titles</u> God gives His Word— "law . . . testimony . . . precepts . . . commandments . . . judgments." Next, observe the <u>characteristics</u> of Scripture— "perfect . . . sure . . . right . . . pure . . . true . . . righteous." Then, observe the <u>benefits</u> it provides—"restoring the

soul . . . making wise the simple . . . rejoicing the heart
. . . enlightening the eyes." Talk about communicating something with effectiveness! No one could name another book or
any other piece of literature that can do such an effective job
in the life of mankind. God is not silent!

Then, as you would expect, David sets forth the *value of Scripture.* He uses two illustrations for the purpose of comparison:

1. Gold . . . fine gold (v. 10). In David's day, this was considered among the most precious of possessions. Man's wealth
was based on the amount of gold he owned. The "fine gold" is
purified gold . . . gold that had been melted down with maxi-
mum impurities and alloy removed.

2. Honey . . . honeycomb (v. 10). Turning from a precious
element to a food, David declares God's Word to be sweeter
than the most delectable of foods. Note that it is not just honey,
but honey flowing from the combs. Makes my mouth water!
Consider honey momentarily.

- It is provided through the work of someone other than
  ourselves; the bee virtually lays it on our platter.

- It is a natural food that doesn't need a lengthy time of di-
  gestion before it goes to work. Immediately, honey provides
  energy.

- Its taste is altogether unique. No other sweetness is quite
  like the rich taste of honey.

Honey—what a fitting analogy!

Read those three things again with God's Word in mind.
Through the efforts of another, we have His Word. It goes to
work immediately upon entering our spiritual system. And no
other piece of literature can even compare with its uniqueness.
No wonder God's Word is said to be "living and active and
sharper than any two-edged sword" (Heb. 4:12).

Finally, verses 11–13 tell us of specific ways God's truth
works within us. Through the Scriptures we are warned of evil
and potential dangers. The individual who really knows (and
applies!) his Bible is kept from numerous sins simply because he

believes God's warning signals. Then, biblical truths assure us of personal <u>reward</u>—"great reward." Furthermore, they provide us with <u>discernment</u>—the ability to know right from wrong. Simple though that may sound, that is one of the signs of maturity, according to Hebrews 5:14. "But solid food is for the mature, who because of practice have their senses trained to discern good and evil."

God's Word also <u>reveals</u> error, sin, presumption, and transgression to those who ponder the pages of Scripture.

CLOSING PRAYER

Verse 14, one of the most familiar verses in the entire Book of Psalms, adequately sums up the psalmist's feelings in the form of a prayer:

> Let the words of my mouth and the meditation of my heart
> Be acceptable in Thy sight,
> O Lord, my rock and my redeemer. [v. 14]

God has revealed Himself. We constantly bask in the sunlight of His presence. We have His Word in our language—clearly printed and conveniently punctuated, bound, and preserved for our use. Added to this, He stands as our Rock (stability, One on whom we can rely) and our Redeemer (deliverance from evil acts, evil men, and our own evil nature).

Stay in the Word this week, my friend. Claim His blessings— dare Him to fulfill His promises. The "words of your mouth" and "meditation of your heart" will take on a whole new pattern of godliness and power. Furthermore, He will no longer seem distant from you or silent to you.

EFLECTIONS
ON DIVINE SILENCE

1. How often we are tempted to think of our God as being distant and silent! According to the song we just studied, He is neither. This week pay closer attention to the natural phenomena that surround you, all of which speak of God's presence. Look up. Look around. Look down. Meditate on the many ways He makes His presence known. Weave those thoughts into your moments of solitude and ask Him to comfort you in tangible ways.

2. Since this song uses gold and honey as illustrations of the value of God's Word, let's focus on both. Perhaps you will want to discuss the analogies with your family or a friend. Eat some honey and remind yourself of its sweetness. Examine the beauty of a gold necklace or ring. Draw a few conclusions of your own. Talk about them.

3. Go back into Psalm 19. Locate the mention of "errors" and "hidden faults" (v. 12) as well as "presumptuous sins" (v. 13). Think about the difference during the week. By the end of the week, talk to the Lord about each in your own life.

PSALM

A Psalm of David.

The Lord is my shepherd,
I shall not want.
He makes me lie down in green
pastures;
He leads me beside quiet waters.
He restores my soul;
He guides me in the paths of
righteousness
For His name's sake.

Even though I walk through the valley of
the shadow of death,
I fear no evil; for Thou art with me;
Thy rod and Thy staff, they comfort me.
Thou dost prepare a table before me in
the presence of my enemies;
Thou hast anointed my head with oil;
My cup overflows.
Surely goodness and lovingkindness will
follow me all the days of my life,
And I will dwell in the house of the Lord
forever. [23:1–6]

THE GRIND OF UNCERTAINTY

No one would deny that Psalm 23 is the most familiar, best-loved portion of the Book of Psalms—perhaps of the entire Bible! It has endeared itself to people in every circumstance of life:

- The soldier in battle, fearing injury and possible death
- The grieving widow standing before a fresh grave, wondering how she can go on with her life
- The guilty wanderer seeking forgiveness and direction
- The lonely stranger longing for love and companionship
- The suffering saint strapped to a bed of pain
- The orphan and the forgotten
- The depressed and the jobless
- The prison inmate and the persecuted
- The prodigal and the divorced

All have felt the stinging daily grind of uncertainty. To each one (and thousands more) Psalm 23 brings solace and peace. When the "chips are down" and our hearts are heaviest, it is to this magnificent "Psalm of the Shepherd" we most often turn. The preschooler knows it by heart, yet it is a silent partner of the retired—and always fitting at a funeral. From the cradle to the grave, Psalm 23 provides timeless comfort and endless assurance for those who lack the secure feeling of God's perpetual presence.

I have observed that few inner battles are more fierce than the daily grind of uncertainty. No doubt you too have encountered one or more of its many faces as you have struggled with a career choice, direction in life, purpose in pain, job security, financial pressures, physical handicaps, relational snags, and a dozen other confusing puzzles not quickly or easily solved.

Because of the popularity of this song and the numerous truths that are hidden in it, we will want to spend more time on it than we have on the others. Therefore, I've chosen not to give a formal outline. Instead we will consider the analogy of sheep to the children of God, the theme of constant provision by our Shepherd-Lord, and an explanation of each verse.

ANALOGY

One cannot read Psalm 23 without realizing that it is written from the viewpoint of a sheep. It is as though a sheep were considering its life among the flock with its shepherd and recording its feelings and observations. Consider some of the analogies between helpless sheep and God's frail children:

1. Sheep lack a sense of direction. Unlike cats and dogs, sheep can get lost easily—even in the familiar environment of their own territory. So it is with believers—we cannot guide ourselves. We must rely completely on the Word of God and the voice of our Shepherd-Savior.

2. Sheep are virtually defenseless. Most animals have a rather effective means of defense—sharp claws; teeth; speed; ability to hide; keenness of smell, sight, and hearing; great strength; ferocity. But sheep are awkward, weak, and ignorant; they have spindle legs and tiny hoofs, and are pitifully slow, even devoid of an angry growl. Defenseless! The only

sure protection for the sheep is the ever-watchful shepherd. So it is with the believer, who is admonished to be strong—"in the Lord" (Eph. 6:10).

3. Sheep are easily frightened. Being ignorant, unimpressive in stature, and very much aware of their weakness, sheep find comfort only in their shepherd's presence and reassuring songs in the night. Psalm 27:1 also refers to this type of Shepherd-Lord relationship which we have with God.

4. Sheep are, by nature, unclean. Other animals lick, scrape, and roll in the grass to cleanse themselves—but not sheep. They will remain filthy indefinitely unless the shepherd cleanses them. We, too, by nature, are unclean and filthy. Apart from our tender Shepherd's cleansing (1 John 1:7–9) we would remain perpetually dirty.

5. Sheep cannot find food or water. While most animals have a keen sense of smell, sheep depend upon their shepherd completely. If left to themselves, sheep will eat poisonous weeds and die—and when one does it the others will follow the leader. Again, as children of God, we are equally dependent.

6. The sheep's wool does not belong to the sheep. While sheep may produce wool, the shepherd owns their wool. All bona fide spiritual production in the life of the Christian belongs to the Lord. The Lord, by means of the Holy Spirit, provides for all such production. In every way, you see, we are indeed "His people and the sheep of His pasture" (Ps. 100:3).

THEME

Like many of the psalms, Psalm 23 states its case in the first verse and simply verifies it in the remainder of the song.

The key thought is this: Because the Lord is my Shepherd, I shall not want for anything—I shall lack nothing! No uncertainty should frighten me. Here is the way the theme of Psalm 23 is played out in the balance of David's famous song:

I shall not lack rest or provision—why?
He makes me lie down in green pastures.
I shall not lack peace—why?
He leads me beside quiet waters.
I shall not lack restoration or encouragement when I faint, fail, or
  fall—why?
He restores my soul.
I shall not lack guidance or fellowship—why?
He guides me in the paths of righteousness.
I shall not lack courage when my way is dark—why?
*Even though I walk through the valley of the shadow of death, I
  fear no evil.*
I shall not lack companionship—why?
For Thou art with me.
I shall not lack constant comfort—why?
Thy rod and Thy staff, they comfort me.
I shall not lack protection or honor—why?
Thou dost prepare a table before me in the presence of my enemies.
I shall not lack power—why?
Thou hast anointed my head with oil.
I shall not lack abundance—why?
My cup overflows.
I shall not lack God's perpetual presence—why?
Surely goodness and mercy shall follow me all the days of my life.
I shall not lack security—why?
And I will dwell in the house of the Lord forever.

EXPLANATION

Although familiar in its form, Psalm 23 develops an unfamiliar metaphor throughout. I am referring to the shepherd-sheep experience. Few people in America have even seen a flock of sheep under a shepherd's care, much less experienced the everyday occurrences common to that mode of life. Because the scene is unfamiliar, many are at a loss to explain this song in its basic sense, for David drew his words from the memory of those years he had spent on the Judean hillside with his father's flock. I suggest you get hold of a book that describes the life of a shepherd—or better still, talk with someone who has worked with sheep. Believe me; the psalm will burst into life for you. No one can adequately enter into the depths of this beloved psalm unless he or she first becomes familiar with the way a shepherd relates to his sheep.

Verse 1

As I've already stated, this verse gives us the theme of the song. But for now I call your attention to two things in this sentence:

1. David refers to God as "the Lord." This is the translation of *Jehovah*—the most respected, loftiest title a Jew could utter. The Hebrews stood in awe before it—it was so holy that they substituted it with some lesser title for God whenever it occurred in their public reading of sacred Scripture. *Jehovah* means "the I AM," the self-existent Being; He who was and is and is to come, who inhabits eternity, who has life in Himself.

F. B. Meyer writes of this title:

> . . . All other life, from the aphid on the rose-leaf to the archangel before the throne, is dependent and derived. All others waste and change and grow old; He only is unchangeably the same. All others are fires, which He supplies with fuel; He alone is self-sustained. This mighty Being is our Shepherd![3]

From our perspective today, the Lord Jesus Christ is the Shepherd of this psalm.

2. David calls Jehovah "*my* Shepherd." To David (the sheep), God was his own, personal Shepherd. Millions of people know that the Lord is *a* Shepherd, but they really don't know that He is *their* Shepherd.

Who, by the way, is *your* Shepherd? In whom do you trust when you are feeling caught in the daily grind of uncertainty? To whom do you turn for direction? You have many choices. Do you go first to your pastor? Your psychologist? Your close friend? Your coach? Your priest? Your teacher? How easy to forget that they are sheep, too! As important and necessary as each of these people may be, they can never take the place of the Good Shepherd in your life. When you finally come to the place where *all* of your life—in all its detail—is placed in Christ's care, you can say with a deep, abiding certainty, "The Lord is *my* Shepherd, I shall not want."

Verse 2

Now the number-one composer of Israel begins to develop the theme he stated in verse 1. He starts with the pastoral picture of sheep under a shepherd's care. I am told that sheep, being stupid animals, frequently are alarmed and actually run over each other, racing away from something that startles them. The shepherd corrects the problem by catching a sheep and gently, yet firmly, forcing it to lie down and feed quietly on the grass beneath its feet. David remembers such an occasion as he says, "He makes me lie down. . . ."

In our hectic, hurried, harassed age in which headache medications have become the best-selling national product, we must occasionally be *made* to lie down by our Shepherd-Savior. When He steps into our helter-skelter world, He often *forces* us to rest. If that has occurred, give thanks—the pastures are green!

This verse concludes with another pleasant picture: "He leads me beside quiet waters." Look at that phrase. Literally, it refers to waters that have been stilled. Mentally capture the peaceful scene. The sheep are weary and worn. They need a long, refreshing drink from the rapid stream nearby. But sheep are instinctively afraid of running water. Perhaps they think that if water should get on their heavy coats of wool, they would become waterlogged and sink beneath the surface of a stream. As a result, even though tired and hot from a blistering day, thirsty sheep will only stand and stare at the fast-flowing stream but never drink. Uncertainty keeps them from needed refreshment.

The shepherd then steps in. With his rod and staff he loosens a few large stones and dams up a place, causing the rushing waters to slow their current. The now quiet waters immediately attract the sheep. In the midst of a rushing stream, the shepherd has provided refreshment for the flock with water he has stilled.

Has your Shepherd done this? Has He recently stepped in and made those busy currents of your life a source of refreshment by stilling them, by bringing order out of chaos? Isn't it true that we frequently receive spiritual refreshment from uncertain circumstances we dreaded most?

Verse 3

"He restores my soul. . . ." *Restoration.* What a full, meaningful term! Again, there is that familiar scene along the hillside. Sheep have a bad habit of wandering. When one is attracted to a clump of grass away from the flock, off he goes, and sometimes he's followed by several other woolly wanderers. Soon, night falls. Lurking in the darkness are hungry wolves, four-legged savages, looking for a supper of mutton! The shepherd counts his sheep, calling them by name.

Realizing he has a wanderer missing, he strikes out to "restore" that wandering member of his flock . . . calling its name and awaiting an answering bleat out in the wilderness beneath the eerie glow of the moon.

Occasionally, one particular young sheep will get into a habit of wandering. Again and again the shepherd will have to go and find the wandering lamb. When such occurs too often, the shepherd will lift the lamb from the thistles and cactus, hold it close, and abruptly break its leg. He will make a splint for the shattered leg and then carry that once-wayward lamb near his heart. That sheep learns a bitter lesson and all the while depends completely upon its shepherd during the period of *restoration.*

Do I write to a wandering sheep? Do my words fall upon one of God's children who has gotten into a habit of drifting from the flock? Let me remind you of one important word—*He.* It is *He,* the Shepherd-Savior who will restore you. He is looking for you if you have strayed away. He is jealous for your love.

He wants you back . . . and I must warn you—He will stop at nothing in order to restore you. God doesn't play games—especially with His wayward woollies!

Finally, verse 3 promises guidance. Look at the last part of this verse. Literally, it means: "He guides me in the right tracks for His name's sake."

The Palestinian shepherd was a master at reading tracks. Many marks and paths sprawled across the rugged terrain. Some were made by wilderness beasts, others by robbers lying in wait. The wind also etched its subtle "track" in the sand. To the untrained, dull eye of the sheep, they all looked alike—like real paths. But they led nowhere. The sheep were wise to follow only their shepherd, who always led them along the "right track." After all, it was the shepherd's reputation that was at stake: ". . . for His name's sake."

The application is obvious. Many voices shout for our attention. Many religions plead for a hearing. Many media ministries beg for the public's involvement (especially our financial support). Many "new doctrines" seduce us to listen . . . and, alas, many are led astray! When we follow our Shepherd, however, we follow along the "right tracks." His written Word gives us the guidance we need so desperately.

The tone changes in the latter half of Psalm 23 . . . but not the Shepherd! From the verdant, fertile slopes and bubbling brooks of verses 2 and 3, we are plunged immediately down into the "valley of the shadow of death"—literally translated the "valley of deep darkness." How does this tie in with verse 3? You'll observe that verse 3 promises that our Shepherd-Savior guides us along "right tracks." Verse 4 is simply saying that one of these tracks or paths winds along the steep, downward valley below. There is a reason for this.

Verse 4

This scene is familiar to those who know the habit of shepherds. Early in the year the flocks graze leisurely in the lowlands, but as summer's sun begins to melt the high mountain snow, the shepherd leads his flock to better grazing land above. This trip inevitably includes some dangerous paths filled with uncertainties and fearful sights. The way is dark, unfamiliar, difficult. The "valley of deep darkness" leads along turbid waters crashing and foaming over jagged rocks. The trees periodically blot out the sunlight and there are serpents coiled to strike as well as hungry wolves lurking in the shadows. But the sheep walking beside his shepherd is secure, though naturally frightened, because the shepherd is near, leading the way, fully aware of the valley's path. Such a scene was as familiar to David as a sheet of music is to an orchestra conductor . . . or a mechanical drawing to an engineer. The ancient shepherd-made-king mentally sifts through those earlier days as a lad in the wilderness with his father's flock and pictures himself as a sheep: "Even though *I* walk through the valley. . . ."

We, as God's sheep, are sometimes led by Him into the valley of darkness, where there is fear, danger, uncertainty, and the unexpected. He knows that the only way we can reach the higher places of Christian experience and maturity is not on the playground of prosperity but in the schoolroom of suffering. Along those dark, narrow, pinching, uncomfortable valleys of difficulty we learn volumes! We keep our courage simply because our Shepherd is leading the way. Perhaps that is what the writer had in mind when he exhorted us to keep ". . . fixing our eyes on Jesus. . . . For consider Him . . . so that you may not grow weary and lose heart" (Heb. 12:2–3).

Notice that the psalmist says because "Thou art with me" he is kept from being afraid. Mark it down, my friend. There is *no* experience, *no* valley (no matter how severe or uncertain) that we must journey alone.

Take special note of what David claims as his source of comfort: the Lord's rod and staff. The shepherd's rod was a symbol of his power. Actually, it was an oak club about two feet in length. It was used to defend the flock against wild beasts. The head of this rod was round, usually whittled from the knot of a tree—in which the shepherd had pounded sharp bits of metal. One expositor remarks:

A skillful shepherd not only swung the club to smash the head of an attacker, but he could also hurl the club like a missile over the heads of his flock to strike a wolf lurking in the distance.[4]

The shepherd, by being well-armed with this heavy club, could deal death-giving blows to a lion or bear or stealthy thief imperiling the safety of one of his charges.

The shepherd's staff was his crook, which was bent or hooked at one end. It provided the shepherd with an instrument for prying a sheep loose from a thicket, pushing branches aside along the narrow path, and pulling wandering sheep out of holes into which they had fallen. He also used it to beat down high grass to drive out snakes and wild beasts. Like the rod, the staff was a symbol of the shepherd's power and strength.

The sheep took comfort in the strength of its shepherd. No need to be uncomfortable with the power of God. We are to find relief and peace of mind in the fact that *He is able.* When surrounded and outnumbered by enemies, it should bring relief to us in realizing that He will use His "rod" and "staff" to protect us.

Verse 5

In spite of the fact that this song has many full and meaningful phrases, the first portion of this verse initially seems difficult to understand. Suddenly, the analogy breaks down. No sheep ever ate at a literal "table" prepared for it. And what does it mean "in the presence of my enemies . . ."? Abruptly, we are transported from the green pastures, the valley, and the rugged mountainside to "a table" in the enemy's presence. The picture may appear to change, but again, the common experience of a shepherd with his flock brings us understanding.

I have Charles W. Slemming to thank for help with this verse. He has done a masterful piece of work in his writings concerning shepherds in the Middle East.[5]

In this case he tells of the shepherd who comes to a new field in which he plans to graze his flock. The shepherd doesn't just turn them loose, he inspects the field for vipers—small brown adders that live under the ground. They frequently pop up out of their tiny holes and nip the sheep on their noses. The bite from these natural enemies sometimes causes an inflammation which can, on occasion, kill the stricken sheep.

Knowing this danger, the shepherd restrains his sheep from a new field (which may be infested) until he can inspect it. He walks up and down, looking for the small holes. Upon finding these holes, he takes a bottle of thick oil from his girdle.

Then, raking down the long grass with his staff, he pours a circle of oil at the top of each viper's hole. Before he leads the sheep into the new, green field, he also spreads the oil over each sheep's head—in that sense he "anoints" them (rubbing their heads) with his oil. When the vipers beneath the surface sense the presence of sheep and attempt to attack from their holes, they are unable to do so. Their smooth bodies cannot pass over the slippery oil—they become prisoners inside their own holes.

The oil on the sheep's head also acts as a repellent, so if a viper does manage to come near, the smell drives the serpent away. Therefore, in a very literal sense, by oiling the vipers' burrows, the shepherd has prepared the table—the meadow— and the sheep are able to graze in abundance right in the enemy's presence.

The Lord does that for His people. He frequently sends us on missions that include some danger and overt peril, but even then we bask in His protective mercy and Spirit-directed security. It is good for us to remember that our Lord prayed *not* that we would be taken "out of the world" but that we might be kept "from the evil one" (John 17:15). God's plan for us is not isolation—it's *insulation*.

We dare not overlook "My cup overflows." This refers not to oil, but to water—cool well water so refreshing to a weary sheep's parched tongue.

When there were no streams, a shepherd quenched his flock's thirst beside a well—rather rare in the wilderness. Some wells were deep—as much as a hundred feet down to the water. To draw the water, the shepherd used a long rope with a leather bucket at the end. Since the bucket held less than a gallon and had to be drawn by hand, then poured into large stone cups beside the well, the process was long and laborious. If the flock numbered a hundred, the shepherd could easily spend two hours or more if he allowed them to drink all they wished. Sheep do not like to get wet—and it was a mark of special kindness to keep the cups filled to the brim so they could drink with ease. Only a kind, considerate shepherd satisfied his thirsty sheep with overflowing cups.

How lavishly our Father provides! What bounty! What abundance! Ephesians 3:20 describes our Shepherd-God as One who does "exceeding abundantly beyond all that we ask or think." Not just barely, but abundantly!

I like the way Haddon Robinson expresses this thought:

> With Him the calf is always the fatted calf; the robe is always the best robe; the joy is unspeakable; and the peace passes understanding. There is no grudging in God's goodness. He does not measure His goodness by drops like a druggist filling a prescription. It comes to us in floods. If only we recognized the lavish abundance of His gifts, what a difference it would make in our lives! If every meal were taken as a gift from His hand, it would be almost a sacrament.[6]

May God give us a fresh realization of the overwhelming abundance He provides. Indeed, our cup overflows.

Verse 6

In his book *The Shepherd Psalm*, F. B. Meyer refers to "goodness and lovingkindness" as our "celestial escort."[7] Another quaint commentator suggests that these are "God's sheepdogs" ever near His flock, ever nipping at our heels, always available.[8] Perhaps that is a fitting analogy, especially when we consider that they "follow" us. Because we are "prone to wander, prone to leave the God we love." He sends His faithful companions out after us—goodness and mercy—kindness and *loving*kindness. Our Lord deals with us so kindly, so graciously. What a difference between God and man! Let *man* go on a search for a wayward soul and there is often bitterness and revenge and impatience in his steps, especially if the search is lengthy. But with God, there is goodness and lovingkindness.

I am convinced that one of the reasons the prodigal son "came to himself" and finally returned home was because of the kind of father he had. There is no magnet with a stronger pull than genuine love. Love has drawn back more wanderers and broken more hard hearts than this world will ever know.

It is fitting, then, that you and I are followed "all the days" of our lives by goodness and lovingkindness. God knows what will best do the job! How varied are our Lord's methods.

> When God wants to drill a man
>   And thrill a man
>   And skill a man,
> When God wants to mold a man
>   To plan the noblest part;
> When He yearns with all His heart
>   To create so great and bold a man
> That all the world shall be amazed,
>   Watch His methods, watch His ways!
>
> How He ruthlessly perfects
>   Whom He royally elects!
> How He hammers him and hurts him,
>   And with mighty blows converts him
> Into trial shapes of clay which
>   Only God understands;
> While his tortured heart is crying
>   And he lifts beseeching hands!
> How He bends but never breaks
>   When his good He undertakes;
> How He uses whom He chooses
>   And with every purpose fuses him;
>   By every act induces him
> To try His splendour out—
>   God knows what He's about![9]

Mark it down, my friend—God knows how to deal with His children. More specifically, He knows how to deal with you. His dealings follow you all the days of your life. Your circumstances *right now* are part of His plan for you.

. . . for it is God who is at work in you, both to will and to work for His good pleasure. [Phil. 2:13]

And we know that God causes all things to work together for good to those who love God, to those who are called according to His purpose. [Rom. 8:28]

This wonderful song concludes with a familiar and comforting thought—"I will dwell in the house of the Lord forever." The psalmist is not referring to a *place* as much as he is to a *Person.* Notice that the Twenty-third Psalm begins and ends with "the Lord." David longed to be in his Lord's house, because he could then be in his Lord's presence.

You see, the ultimate goal in David's heart was a face-to-face relationship with His Lord forever. Instead of vague uncertainty, he had confidence. We Christians will enjoy a never-ending fellowship with God the moment we draw our last earthly breath. What assurance!

That is exactly what Jesus Christ promises those who believe in Him . . . not merely "I hope so" but "I know!" In Him we truly have everything we need.

EFLECTIONS ON UNCERTAINTY

1. Meditate on the analogy of the shepherd and his flock of sheep. All week long, think of the Lord as your Shepherd. Give Him thanks for meeting your every need. List a few of them here:

   _____

   _____

   _____

   _____

   _____

2. Have you felt uncertain lately? Maybe a little insecure about the future? Does some "valley of deep darkness" stretch out in front of you? Spend at least five minutes each day this week in prayer. If you can find a place to be all alone so you can get on your knees, do that. Tell God all that is on your heart. Hold nothing back.

3. Goodness and lovingkindness . . . "God's sheepdogs." Have they been staying near you lately? Pick up the phone several times this week and affirm a family member or friend. Remind each one that the Lord's goodness and mercy are keeping watch over them day and night. You might mention the source of your encouragement. Psalm 23 never fails to bring a special touch of comfort.

A Psalm of David.

Vindicate me, O Lord, for I have
    walked in my integrity;
    And I have trusted in the Lord
    without wavering.
Examine me, O Lord, and try me;
Test my mind and my heart.
For Thy lovingkindness is before my
    eyes,
And I have walked in Thy truth.
I do not sit with deceitful men,
Nor will I go with pretenders.
I hate the assembly of evildoers,
And I will not sit with the wicked.
I shall wash my hands in innocence,
And I will go about Thine altar, O Lord,
That I may proclaim with the voice of
    thanksgiving,
And declare all Thy wonders.

O Lord, I love the habitation of Thy
    house,
And the place where Thy glory dwells.
Do not take my soul away along with
    sinners,
Nor my life with men of bloodshed,
In whose hands is a wicked scheme,
And whose right hand is full of bribes.
But as for me, I shall walk in my
    integrity;
Redeem me, and be gracious to me.
My foot stands on a level place;
In the congregations I shall bless the
    Lord.   [26:1–12]

THE GRIND OF MISTREATMENT

If I were asked to give a popular title to this song, it would be: "How to Do Right When You've Been Done Wrong."

We have all been "done wrong," haven't we? Maybe that describes your circumstance right now: an intolerable working situation; a husband, wife, parent, or child who takes advantage of you even when you treat him (or her) kindly; a friend who has turned against you due to a misunderstanding of something you did with only the purest of motives. Such feelings grind away at our peace so severely we wonder how we can continue. Whatever the mistreatment you are having to endure, please accept this warning: DON'T BECOME BITTER! DON'T BACKSLIDE!

The whole thrust of David's ancient composition, according to verse 1, has to do with some undeserved wrong he was enduring—and his determination to trust in his Lord "without wavering." Read the first verse again, only this time more slowly, to sense the feeling behind it: "Vindicate me, O Lord, for I have walked in my integrity; / And I have trusted in the Lord without wavering."

Descriptive phrase, "without wavering." The Hebrew verb which is translated "wavering" means "to slip, slide, totter, shake." David is saying that in spite of the daily grind of mistreatment he was living under, he was so determined to trust the Lord he would not slip or slide under the load! That explains why he begins the psalm with such an emotional plea: "Vindicate me, O Lord." You see, by his own honest admission, he was right; he was walking in integrity. That was not pride; he was stating a fact to his Lord. As he continues, he reviews the specific things that kept him upright while under unfair attacks.

Let's move through the song, keeping its theme in mind. As we do so, we will uncover six things David mentions which kept him (and will keep us) from slipping into bitterness and resentment during times of mistreatment.

1. Be open before the Lord: "Examine me, O Lord, and try me; / Test my mind and my heart" (v. 2). In three different ways David encourages His Lord to prove his inner being: "Examine . . . try . . . test. . . ."

These three English terms represent three different Hebrew terms. The first one is *bah-chan*, meaning "to examine, prove, scrutinize." It is clearly portrayed in Psalm 139:23–24 by the word *search*.

> Search me, O God, and know my heart;
> Try me and know my anxious thoughts;
> And see if there be any hurtful way in me,
> And lead me in the everlasting way.

Literally, he is asking God to "make an examination" of his inner being, to "scrutinize" him through and through.

The next term, translated "try" in verse 2, is the Hebrew *nah-sah*, which means to "test, try, prove." Deuteronomy 8:2 uses the term with its intensive (Piel) stem, meaning "an intensive test":

> And you shall remember all the way which the Lord your God has led you in the wilderness these forty years, that He might humble you, *testing* you, to know what was in your heart, whether you would keep His commandments or not. [Emphasis mine.]

God put the Israelites to an intensive test so that the real condition of their heart might be exposed.

The third term, rendered "test" in verse 2, is yet another Hebrew verb—*tzah-raff*. This is such a vivid word! Literally, it means "to smelt, refine, test." Of the thirty-two times in the Old

Testament it appears in verb form, twenty-two of those times it is linked with the activity of refining gold or silver, removing the dross and impurities.

Do you grasp the principle? When wrong comes your way, be open before the Lord. Invite Him (1) to make an internal search and examination of your life, for the purpose of determining your character, (2) to undertake an intensive, in-depth process of revealing to you the real condition of your heart, and (3) to melt and refine you . . . remove the dross and impurities which this particular mistreatment has brought to the surface. In other words, openly welcome His internal divine surgery on your innermost being. Look upon the wrong that comes your way as a choice opportunity to become increasingly more transparent and pure before the Lord. Ask Him for insight—for a full disclosure of your inner person.

Consider James 1:2–4 from J. B. Phillips' paraphrase:

> When all kinds of trials and temptations crowd into your lives, my brothers, don't resent them as intruders, but welcome them as friends! Realize that they come to test your faith and to produce in you the quality of endurance. But let the process go on until that endurance is fully developed, and you will find you have become men of mature character with the right sort of independence.

2. Remember his love and continue to obey His word: "For Thy lovingkindness is before my eyes, / And I have walked in Thy truth" (Ps. 26:3).

That statement implies two very subtle yet common temptations that occur when mistreatment comes our way:

a. We doubt God's love.
b. We drift into disobedience.

David declares, "Thy lovingkindness is before my eyes. . . ." How descriptive! He is admitting whatever comes before him; he looks at it through the lovingkindness of His Lord. It was God's lovingkindness that served as his mental "filter." Then, lest he drift into the ugly yet common temptation to strike back, he states that it is "in Thy truth" he continues to walk. Do you see this? His eyes are on the Lord's *love* for him . . . and his guide through the maze of mistreatment is the Lord's *truth.*

Are you aware of the best proof of love? It is obedience. Our Lord reminds us of that in John 14:15, 21, 23:

> "If you love Me, you will keep My commandments." [v. 15]

> "He who has My commandments and keeps them, he it is who loves Me; and he who loves Me shall be loved by My Father, and I will love him, and will disclose Myself to him." [v. 21]

> Jesus answered and said to him, "If anyone loves Me, he will keep My word; and my Father will love him, and We will come to him, and make Our abode with him." [v. 23]

If you are confident that someone really loves you, you will neither doubt nor drift in your response. Instead, you will find great delight in pleasing that individual. There is nothing quite like love to motivate us from within.

3. Refuse the temptation to get even:

> I do not sit with deceitful men,
> Nor will I go with pretenders.
> I hate the assembly of evildoers,
> And I will not sit with the wicked. [vv. 4–5]

This matter of getting involved with the wrong crowd is a byproduct of doubting and drifting. We are especially vulnerable to this trap when we have been mistreated. You will always find a group of people who will encourage your compromising and rebelling—those who say, "Why put up with that? Listen, you've got your rights; *fight back!*"

Consider David's plight. Perhaps it was when Saul hunted for him out of jealousy. David did not deserve such unfair treatment. Surely he had well-meaning friends who encouraged him to retaliate, to "get back" at Saul. On more than one occasion he deliberately resisted getting even, though a few of his friends urged him to do so. David felt that if the Lord was able to protect him, He was able to handle his enemies as well. (You may wish to stop and read 1 Samuel 24:1–20 and 26:6–12).

Then again, David may have written this song while he was going through the torment of those days when his favored son Absalom conspired against him and unfairly attempted to take the throne of Israel away from him (2 Sam. 15:1–6). This finally resulted in David's having to run for his life. Wisely, even though mistreated, David never did attempt to "get back" at his son or listen to the carnal advice of men around him.

Perhaps you have fallen prey to the unwise counsel of wrong associates. In the words of Psalm 26, when this happens you "sit with deceitful [worthless] men" and "go with pretenders [hypocrites]." Consider also the words of 1 Corinthians 15:33: "Do not be deceived: 'Bad company corrupts good morals.'"

How very true! You cannot identify yourself with wrong associates and walk away unaffected. The point is clear: Do not let mistreatment cause you to turn to the godless crowd or adopt their way of handling things. It may seem logical, but getting even often backfires; and it never glorifies God!

4. <u>Maintain a positive attitude</u>:

> I shall wash my hands in innocence,
> And I will go about Thine altar, O Lord,
> That I may proclaim with the voice of thanksgiving,
> And declare all Thy wonders. [vv. 6–7]

David is so concerned that his heart remain right, he refers to "washing his hands" and staying near "Thine altar." These are word pictures familiar to the Jews. In Exodus 30:17–21 the laver (basin) of bronze that belonged in the Tabernacle is mentioned. It was used for the washing of the priests' hands and feet before they approached the altar to minister. If they failed to wash, they were killed by the Lord!

David picks up that very important and serious principle in his song on mistreatment and applies it to his situation. He stayed very near his Lord at this time, making sure his sins were confessed and his heart attitude was clean. By doing so, he remained positive. This did not guarantee, however, that the mistreatment suddenly ended. Listen to Psalm 73:13-14:

> Surely in vain I have kept my heart pure,
> And washed my hands in innocence;
> For I have been stricken all day long,
> And chastened every morning.

Let's not think that a clean, godly life is always immediately blessed with pleasant circumstances. But rest assured that maintaining the proper relationship with the Lord is still the very best way to endure mistreatment.

Also note that Psalm 26:7 refers to an attitude of *thanksgiving*. David actually proclaimed words of thanksgiving to God for being mistreated. Talk about a positive attitude! The crucial test of giving thanks in everything (1 Thessalonians 5:18) occurs when we suffer mistreatment. That is the supreme test on our attitude of thanksgiving.

I'm thinking of another account much later in biblical times that has to do with the courageous, first-century apostles who were thrown in jail for preaching Christ and doing His work publicly (Acts 5:17-18). After being humiliated and rebuked for their convictions by the religious leaders (v. 28), they were beaten unmercifully and warned not to continue in their ministry of teaching, healing, and casting out demons (v. 40). What is incredible to me is their indomitable, positive attitude:

> So they went on their way from the presence of the Council, rejoicing that they had been considered worthy to suffer shame for His name. And every day, in the temple and from house to house, they kept right on teaching and preaching Jesus as the Christ. [vv. 41-42]

There is every temptation to forget to give God thanks for the privilege of being His example to others when we have been "done wrong." Learn to respond *first* with a genuine "thanks, Lord," when some undeserved attack comes your way. If you do this, you will be unique. Furthermore, a positive attitude clears our minds of needless debris, mental garbage which never fails to counteract all scriptural counsel.

5. Be faithful in public worship: "O Lord, I love the habitation of Thy house, / And the place where Thy glory dwells" (v. 8).

David was quite a man! As I read this verse, I can see why he was known as "a man after God's own heart." Even while he was under the pile, feeling more like a punching bag than a child of the Lord, he remained faithful to the place where he could sense God's glory—the tabernacle (v. 8). You must pause and read three stanzas from three ancient Psalms: 27:4, 65:4, and 84:10. To him, worship was no religious habit, no ritualistic, boring process; it was something essential, something vital. When undergoing mistreatment, David looked up in worship.

Unfortunately, we live in a day of de-emphasis regarding the value and necessity of public worship. I realize that some churches may fail to point the worshiper to the living Christ and to teach His marvelous Word. But this does not mean that all churches and all public worship gatherings are to be ignored! Hebrews 10:23–25 leaves us no option—we are to assemble together for the purpose of mutual stimulation toward the expression of love and good deeds . . . for encouragement! This is so important when undergoing mistreatment. We *need* each other. Christian friend, do not neglect this God-ordained, healthy expression of your faith.

Let me add one more thought here. Show me a believer who consistently neglects the regular services of a church that faithfully preaches and teaches the Word, and I'll show you one whose cutting edge on spiritual things is getting dull—one who is losing ground, spiritually speaking. I detect from my reading of the Book of Acts that the healthy yet persecuted believers mentioned therein absolutely craved every opportunity to meet and worship together. What a healthy example to follow!

6. Patiently stand and wait for relief:

> Do not take my soul away along with sinners,
> Nor my life with men of bloodshed,

In whose hands is a wicked scheme,
And whose right hand is full of bribes.
But as for me, I shall walk in my integrity;
Redeem me, and be gracious to me.
My foot stands on a level place;
In the congregations I shall bless the Lord. [vv. 9–12]

There is something about human nature that prompts us to get busy and quickly work things out. In this section of his song, David implies that such was the activity of those around him. The majority said that they "wouldn't stand for such a thing." All sorts of "wicked schemes" and hands "full of bribes" were implemented by others. Not David!

"But as for me. . . ." In Hebrew, the pronoun is extremely emphatic: "But *me* . . . as for *me!*"

He wanted it known that he wasn't going to panic and, like the majority, get all involved in those anxieties and ulcer-producing activities of self-vindication. No way! What does he say?

. . . I shall walk in my integrity;
Redeem me, and be gracious to me.
My foot stands on a level place; . . .

There's a calmness, a quiet confidence in those words.

- As for my present course: "I . . . walk in integrity."
- As for my defense: "Redeem me . . . be gracious to me."
- As for my inner feelings: "My foot stands. . . ."

What stability! What patience! What assurance and faith! No sleepless nights, no doubts—just patient waiting.

Look back at that term *redeem*. The Hebrew is *rah-dah*, meaning "to ransom, deliver." It is a term of relief—as if in exile. It is the idea of delivering someone from terrible stress and even death. And don't miss that intriguing phrase in verse 12: "My foot stands on a level place. . . ." What interests me is the "level place." It is from a single Hebrew term, *mee-shore*, which can be traced back to the verb *yah-shaar*, meaning "to be smooth, straight." The first term, *mee-shore*, means "level country, a plain." It conveys the idea of a place that has a commanding view—a broad range of vision, in contrast to a place that is down in a deep gorge all shut in.

Do you get the picture? David is pleased to wait quietly on the Lord and remain totally objective. When he waits for God to deliver him, he maintains a panoramic perspective; he is able to look upon the entire process from God's viewpoint, not from his own limited human perspective. In brief, he is able to maintain *wisdom*. We'll examine that term much more in depth when we come to the sayings in Scripture—the Proverbs of Solomon.

You probably anticipate the application. When we patiently wait on the Lord's deliverance, we are able to stay calm and wise in the midst of mistreatment. We can count on Him to be gracious and to deliver us at the right time. All the while, waiting enables us to keep His perspective.

Look back over the six things that will make mistreatment bearable:

1. Be open before the Lord.
2. Remember His love. Continue to obey His Word.
3. Refuse the temptation to get even.
4. Maintain a positive attitude.
5. Be faithful in public worship.
6. Patiently stand and wait for relief.

Do you remember the words of 1 Peter 2:19–21?

> For this finds favor, if for the sake of conscience toward God a man bears up under sorrows when suffering unjustly. For what credit is there if, when you sin and are harshly treated, you endure it with patience? But if when you do what is right and suffer for it you patiently endure it, this finds favor with God. For you have been called for this purpose, since Christ also suffered for you, leaving you an example for you to follow in His steps.

May the thoughts from David's ancient song equip you to do right when you've been done wrong.

EFLECTIONS
ON MISTREATMENT

1. Think of the last time you were mistreated. Now then . . . answer these questions very honestly. They may hurt, but they deserve an answer:

   a. Have you completely released the offense to God?
   b. Do you hold a grudge?
   c. Are you waiting for the right moment to get even?
   d. Is your walk with the Lord stronger than ever before?

2. Look back over the six principles from David's song. Are you at peace with each one or do you need to come to terms with one or two? Be completely honest before the Lord. Hold nothing back.

3. Do you know of someone right now who is enduring the grind of mistreatment? If so, why not write a note of encouragement? You might even share a couple of thoughts from your reflections this week. Go easy. Remember the importance of tact. People being mistreated can be pretty fragile souls.

PSALM

A Psalm of David.

The Lord is my light and my
   salvation;
   Whom shall I fear?
   The Lord is the defense of my
   life;
Whom shall I dread?
When evildoers came upon me to devour
   my flesh,
My adversaries and my enemies, they
   stumbled and fell.
Though a host encamp against me,
My heart will not fear;
Though war arise against me,
In spite of this I shall be confident.

One thing I have asked from the Lord,
   that I shall seek:
That I may dwell in the house of the Lord
   all the days of my life,
To behold the beauty of the Lord,
And to meditate in His temple.
For in the day of trouble He will conceal
   me in His tabernacle;
In the secret place of His tent He will
   hide me;
He will lift me up on a rock.
And now my head will be lifted up
   above my enemies around me;
And I will offer in His tent sacrifices
   with shouts of joy;
I will sing, yes, I will sing praises to the
   Lord.

Hear, O Lord, when I cry with my voice,
And be gracious to me and answer me.
When Thou didst say, "Seek My face," my
    heart said to Thee,
"Thy face, O Lord, I shall seek."
Do not hide Thy face from me,
Do not turn Thy servant away in anger;
Thou hast been my help;
Do not abandon me nor forsake me,
O God of my salvation!
For my father and my mother have
    forsaken me,
But the Lord will take me up.

Teach me Thy way, O Lord,
And lead me in a level path,
Because of my foes.
Do not deliver me over to the desire of
    my adversaries;
For false witnesses have risen against me,
And such as breathe out violence.
I would have despaired unless I had
    believed that I would see the goodness
    of the Lord
In the land of the living.
Wait for the Lord;
Be strong, and let your heart take
    courage;
Yes, wait for the Lord.   [27:1–14]

THE GRIND OF FEAR

One of the most paralyzing problems in all of life is fear. Our fears are directed in so many areas: fear of the unknown, fear of calamity, fear of sickness, disease, and death, fear of people, fear of losing our jobs, fear of enemy attacks, fear of being misunderstood . . . or rejected . . . or criticized . . . or forgotten . . . or (as we just considered) being mistreated. What makes matters worse is that at times the very thing we feared occurs. Sometimes it is worse than we anticipated! I've known times when I felt virtually paralyzed with feelings of panic. As fear gets a firm grip on us, we become its victim.

This reminds me of a college friend of mine who worked several summers ago on a construction crew, building a hospital in Texas. He was assigned to the twelfth story and was given the job of helping a welder who was welding the flooring structure made of huge, steel beams. So scared of falling, my friend literally shook with fear every day, though he admitted it to no one. One hot afternoon the welder looked up and noticed the man shaking in his boots. He yelled, "Are you scared, son?" The student stuttered "—s-s-s-scared! I've been t-t-t-trying to tell you for t-t-t-two weeks that I q-q-q-quit!"

Frozen with fear!

If fear has become your daily grind, Psalm 27 should prove very important—for it is a song designed to take the pain out of that dreadful grind.

OUTLINE

Go back and read the fourteen verses of Psalm 27 once again . . . this time much more slowly and thoughtfully, as if for the first time in your life.

Did you notice a contrast? I'm referring to the great difference between the beginning of the song (vv. 1–6) and its ending (vv. 7–14).

The first half is filled with praise, confidence, victory, and even singing. But the last half is filled with needs—actually it is a grocery list of requests. Look at the expressions David uses in his composition:

Verse 7: "Hear, O Lord . . . and answer me."

Verse 8: "Thy face, O Lord, I shall seek."

Verse 9: "Do not hide . . . Do not turn . . . Do not abandon me nor forsake me."

Verse 11: "Teach me . . . O Lord."

There is a tone of utter dependence in those ancient lyrics.

This gives us the overall layout and helps us come up with an outline.

I. Declaration of Praise (vv. 1– 6)
II. Petition for Needs (vv. 7–13)
III. Exhortation to Wait (v. 14)

What do you do when fear increases and you want to hold up under it? How do you handle such trials? We would do well to follow David's example. He first declared what he knew (vv. 1–6). He then expressed what he needed (vv. 7–13). And finally . . . he encouraged himself to wait (v. 14). Let's examine the song from that threefold perspective.

DECLARATION OF PRAISE

The key to the entire song is verse 1. It consists of two similar sentences, each ending with questions having obvious answers:

"The Lord is my light . . . my salvation . . . the defense of my life." Interestingly, David says Jehovah *is* all of this. He doesn't simply *give* these things. In other words, the psalmist laid claim upon God Himself rather than His works. David knew Jehovah personally. To him, the Lord was a very personal, ever-present Friend and Helper. God was not some distant Deity—an impersonal, abstract, theological Being who hid Himself above the clouds. No, He was David's intimate Companion.

Because of the Lord's presence (which meant more to David than anything else), the songwriter asks: "Whom shall I fear . . . whom shall I dread?"

Here the Hebrew term for *fear* is a common one: *yah-rah*. But the term for *dread* (*phah-chad*) meaning "to be in awe, to be filled with dread" is less common. The Lord God was so significant, so impressive, so overwhelmingly important to David that no other one and no other thing made him stand in awe.

I find it encouraging that Psalm 23 declares, "I shall not want" and Psalm 26 states, "I shall not slide" (KJV). And now Psalm 27 says, I "will not fear." In each case it is because of the personal presence and provisions of Jehovah-God. And by the way, how personal is your Lord? If He is distant, if you feel He is removed, I can assure you that fear is fast becoming a daily grind.

Let's look now at verses 2–3:

> When evildoers came upon me to devour my flesh,
> My adversaries and my enemies, they stumbled and fell.
> Though a host encamp against me,
> My heart will not fear;
> Though war arise against me,
> In spite of this I shall be confident.

As the writer moves on into the song, he enumerates the specific occasions of potential fear: "*evildoers . . . adversaries . . . enemies . . . a host . . . war.*"

Dark scene! And you'll notice that these things weren't mere possibilities; they were realities. He says, "when" not "if."

I hope you are realistic enough to remember that conflicts, criticisms, trials, and afflictions are not the exception but the norm. It is not correct for us to think, *if Satan attacks* . . . but rather *when he attacks*. . . . Christians should be the most realistic, well-informed people on earth. David exemplifies this as he says, "When evildoers came upon me. . . ."

Before leaving the second and third verses, let's take note of two other observations. First, look at the intensity of the conflict: The evildoers came "to devour"; the host (v. 3) had come to "encamp against me"; war had risen "against me." This was no slight affliction. Second, look at the last phrase of verse 3. ". . . In spite of this I shall be confident." The Hebrew says, literally, "I *am* confident!" Danger was imminent. Pressure was mounting. Severe days were ahead. He had every reason to be shaking in his sandals like my friend on the twelfth floor. But he was standing firm!

The Hebrew term used by David and translated "confident" does not mean self-reliant nor brave, humanly speaking. In Hebrew it means "to trust, to be secure, to have assurance." Its Arabic counterpart is picturesque: "to throw oneself down upon one's face, to lie upon the ground." The point I want to get across is that the source of David's confidence and stability was not his own strength—but God. His Lord was his only foundation for rocklike stability. What an unshakable foundation!

When pressure mounts, when a groundswell of fear invites panic, to whom do you turn? In whom do you trust? This song offers abundant reassurance. Pressure and potential fear are reminders to fall back on our Lord. "The arm of flesh will fail you, ye dare not trust your own," says the grand old hymn ("Stand Up, Stand Up for Jesus") by George Duffield.

While living under intense pressure and difficulty, the missionary to inland China, Hudson Taylor, once wrote:

> It does not matter how great the pressure is. What really matters is where the pressure lies—whether it comes between you and God, or whether it presses you nearer His heart.[10]

Verses 4–6 revolve around the idea of David's desire to maintain constant, intimate fellowship with his Lord:

One thing I have asked from the Lord, that I shall seek:
That I may dwell in the house of the Lord all the days of my life,
To behold the beauty of the Lord,
And to meditate in His temple.
For in the day of trouble He will conceal me in His tabernacle;
In the secret place of His tent He will hide me;
He will lift me up on a rock.
And now my head will be lifted up above my enemies around
    me;
And I will offer in His tent sacrifices with shouts of joy;
I will sing, yes, I will sing praises to the Lord.

Observe the repeated references to Jehovah's house, His temple, tabernacle, and tent. These are poetic expressions of being in the place of contact with the Lord. The results of maintaining this fellowship are spelled out:

. . . He will conceal me . . . He will hide me . . . He will lift me up . . . I will offer . . . sacrifices . . . I will sing praises to the Lord.

Did you notice that the first-person-singular pronoun is frequently used? It is woven through these verses—I, me, my. This is the testimony of David *alone.* This is a diary, as it were, of a man's private life, his personal struggles with life's daily grinds. This is not David on display, it is David all alone. We are what we are when we are alone. As has often been said, "Character is what we are when no one is looking."

I also observe that David says: "I will sing, yes, I will sing praises." This is the result of maintaining a close walk with the Lord. Turn to Ephesians 5. Verse 18 is a command ". . . be filled with the Spirit." In other words, allow the Holy Spirit to control your life—your thinking, motives, attitudes, activity. This is vertical fellowship at its best! And then Ephesians 5 goes on to describe the horizontal results of being Spirit-controlled:

Verse 19: a melodious heart—singing!

Verse 20: a thankful attitude—giving thanks!

Verse 21: a submissive spirit—be subject to one another!

When was the last time you burst forth all alone in song? I think it is sad that the Christian's song is seldom heard outside the church building. Living in fellowship with the Lord should bring forth spontaneous melodies throughout the day and night. Let's *sing* our faith!

PETITION FOR NEEDS

Hear, O Lord, when I cry with my voice,
And be gracious to me and answer me.
When Thou didst say, "Seek My face," my heart said to Thee,
"Thy face, O Lord, I shall seek."
Do not hide Thy face from me,
Do not turn Thy servant away in anger;
Thou hast been my help;
Do not abandon me nor forsake me,
O God of my salvation!
For my father and my mother have forsaken me,
But the Lord will take me up.

Teach me Thy way, O Lord,
And lead me in a level path,
Because of my foes,
Do not deliver me over to the desire of my adversaries;
For false witnesses have risen against me,
And such as breathe out violence. [vv. 7–12]

Rather than digging into these verses one by one, let's view them altogether. I want you to take special note of the strong imperatives (the commands) in these verses.

Verse 7: "Hear . . . be gracious . . . answer me!"

Verse 9: "Do not hide thy face . . . Do not turn . . . Do not abandon . . . nor forsake me!"

Verse 11: "Teach me . . . lead me!"

Verse 12: "Do not deliver me over to . . . my adversaries!"

I do not find David kicking back, yawning, and uttering a half-hearted request. I read boldness here, a determined, positive approach to God. Here is a respectful series of commands. With unguarded, unrestrained fervency, the songwriter declares his requests. It is this kind of prayer that is needed today.

Listen to three other verses on the same subject:

> Let us therefore draw near with confidence to the throne of grace, that we may receive mercy and may find grace to help in time of need. [Heb. 4:16]

> The effective prayer of a righteous man can accomplish much. [James 5:16]

> Be anxious for nothing, but in everything by prayer and supplication with thanksgiving let your requests be made known to God. [Phil. 4:6]

As I read such statements, I am reminded of the hesitancy, the lack of fervency and confident boldness in our prayers. Christian friend—ask as though you mean it! Our Lord is pleased when we ask without doubting.

Before turning to the final stanza of David's song, let me ask you to glance back at verse 10. "For my father and my mother have forsaken me, / But the Lord will take me up."

Sandwiched within the commands we just considered is a brief, private admission from David's heart. His parents, for some unrevealed reason, had "forsaken" him. The original Hebrew term means "to leave, desert, abandon." It is this same term that is used in Psalm 22:1, a prophetic statement from the Messiah's lips yet to be uttered from His cross: "My God, my God, why hast Thou forsaken me?" I find it intriguing that David's own parents had turned their backs on their son, even though he was a godly man. Equally interesting is David's security as he declares, "But the Lord will take me up."

Have you ever read Isaiah 49:15–16? What hope it offers!

> Can a woman forget her nursing child,
> And have no compassion on the son of her womb?
> Even these may forget, but I will not forget you.
> Behold, I have inscribed you on the palms of My hands.

God says that mothers may forget their infant babies, but the Lord does not forget one of His.

Have you been forsaken? Have your parents turned against you even though you have tried to maintain a healthy relationship with them? Do they misread your messages? Are they on a different wavelength? Try not to become bitter. Claim the security your Lord promises you. You have nothing to fear because you have Him who has conquered fear. His care is more consistent than that of your parents.

EXHORTATION TO WAIT

"Wait for the Lord; / Be strong, and let your heart take courage; / Yes, wait for the Lord" (v. 14). What a fitting conclusion! David levels an exhortation to himself—wait! He realizes that the pressure would not suddenly leave, nor his enemies do an about-face and run immediately after he rose from his knees. He is realistic enough to know that anything worth having is worth waiting for. So he tells himself to relax . . . to enter into God's rest . . . to cease from his own works (stop and read Hebrews 4:9–11). Strength and courage are developed during a trial, not after it is over.

Look at this term *wait.* It is from the Hebrew verb *kah-wah,* meaning "to twist, stretch." The noun form means "line, cord, thread." A vivid picture emerges. It is a verb describing the making of a strong, powerful rope or cord by twisting and weaving ourselves so tightly around the Lord that our weaknesses and frail characteristics are replaced by His power and unparalleled strength. It describes very literally the truth of what has been termed the "exchanged life." As we wait, our weakness is exchanged for His strength.

Isaiah 40:31 uses this same term: "Yet those who wait for the Lord will gain new strength. . . ."

Philippians 4:13 now takes on new meaning: "I can do all things through Him [literally 'in Him'] who strengthens me."

If you are waiting for God to work this week, keep on waiting! In the wait there will come strength and courage. I urge

you to read and review the truths in Psalm 27 each time you
are tempted to be afraid. Don't become paralyzed and ineffec-
tive. Out with the grind of fear! Look upon each threatening
circumstance as an opportunity to grow in your faith, rather
than to retreat.

First: Declare what you know . . . claim it!

Second: Express what you need . . . boldly!

Third: Wait . . . twist yourself around the strands of
           His strength . . . and relax!

How can you? By remembering that He cares for you.

REFLECTIONS
ON FEAR

1. For the next few minutes, focus on the thought of *fear*. What, exactly, is it? Is it ever healthy? When? Are you often fearful? Why? Does fear ever lead to dread? How?

2. I wrote about pressures when we were examining the third verse in David's Twenty-seventh Psalm. Take an extremely honest look at your life. Do you live most of your days under pressure? During this week, work on a plan that will help decrease your intensity. Be specific. Spell out ways to keep yourself out of that trap.

3. Waiting, which calls for patience, is not a quick-'n'-easy discipline, is it? Focus your attention on something you cannot "fix"—something you are forced to wait for God to work out. Use the space below and write it down:

_____

_____

Look at what you wrote down. Think about it. Visualize it. Is the Lord able to handle it? Several days this week, connect with Him in prayer. Ask Him to calm your motor as you wait for Him to work. Promise Him you'll stay out of it! Wrap your weakness in His cords of strength . . . and wait for Him to work on your behalf.

When He does, give Him all the glory!

A Psalm of David. A Maskil.

How blessed is he whose
transgression is forgiven,
Whose sin is covered!
How blessed is the man to
whom the Lord does not
impute iniquity,
And in whose spirit there is no deceit!

When I kept silent about my sin, my
body wasted away
Through my groaning all day long.
For day and night Thy hand was heavy
upon me;
My vitality was drained away as with the
fever-heat of summer.   [Selah.
I acknowledged my sin to Thee,
And my iniquity I did not hide;
I said, "I will confess my transgressions
to the Lord";
And Thou didst forgive the guilt of my
sin.   [Selah.
Therefore, let everyone who is godly pray
to Thee in a time when Thou mayest
be found;

Surely in a flood of great waters they
    shall not reach him.
Thou art my hiding place; Thou dost
    preserve me from trouble;
Thou dost surround me with songs of
    deliverance.   [Selah.

I will instruct you and teach you in the
    way which you should go;
I will counsel you with My eye upon you.
Do not be as the horse or as the mule
    which have no understanding,
Whose trappings include bit and bridle to
    hold them in check,
Otherwise they will not come near to
    you.
Many are the sorrows of the wicked;
But he who trusts in the Lord,
    lovingkindness shall surround him.
Be glad in the Lord and rejoice you
    righteous ones,
And shout for joy all you who are upright
    in heart.   [32:1–11]

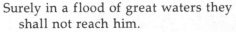

THE GRIND OF AN UNFORGIVEN CONSCIENCE

The conscience may be invisible but it is certainly not inactive! Who hasn't been kept awake by its pleadings? With incredible regularity, an unforgiven conscience can rob us of an appetite as well as drive us to distraction.

Do you remember Edgar Allan Poe's searching story, "The Tell-Tale Heart"? The main character has committed murder. Unable to escape the haunting guilt of his deed, he begins to hear the heartbeat of the victim he has buried in his basement. A cold sweat covers him as the beat-beat-beat goes on, relentlessly. Ultimately, it becomes clear that the pounding which drove the man mad was not in the grave down below but in his own chest. So it is with an unforgiven conscience.

The ancient songwriter David was no stranger to this maddening malady. As we shall soon discover, he became increasingly more physically ill and emotionally distraught the longer he refused to come to terms with the enormity of his grinding guilt. Only forgiveness can take the grind away.

As we begin to read through this song, two things catch the eye even before we get to verse one. First, we notice this is a Psalm of David. It is a song the man David was led to write . . . under the inspiration of the Spirit of God. So, at the outset let's remember that the song he writes is somehow descriptive of David's personal experience. Second, we notice this is a *Maskil*, a term that is unfamiliar to us. *Maskil* is a transliterated Hebrew word that appears before thirteen of the songs in this ancient hymnbook of the Hebrews. Most likely it is from *sah-kaal*, a Hebrew verb meaning "to be prudent, circumspect, wise—to have insight." According to my English dictionary *insight* means "the act or power to see into a situation." Putting all this together we understand that the Thirty-second Psalm is designed to give its readers wisdom and insight when dealing with certain situations.

The situation in this case is the grind that accompanies a conscience that lacks forgiveness. Psalm 51 should be tied in with Psalm 32. Both were written after David's adultery with Bathsheba and his attempt to cover up his sin by having her husband Uriah set up to lose his life on the battlefield. Of the two, Psalm 51 was probably written first, *during* the anguish of guilt under which David suffered so severely. Psalm 32 was written *after* the anguish, after his forgiveness had been secured and his peace of mind had been restored. So, the theme of Psalm 32 could be "The Blessedness of Forgiveness," and how it can be achieved. We learn right away that this song is very relevant . . . for we live in a world filled with people living under self-imposed guilt who are deeply in need of forgiveness.

OUTLINE

Read the eleven verses once again, only this time a little more slowly. Try to enter into the feelings of David. It is obvious that he is joyful at the outset, rejoicing in his present state of forgiveness (vv. 1–2). He then falls into a reflective mood as he thinks back to days past (vv. 3–5). Twice during this section of the song, he adds the word *Selah,* a musical notation meaning "pause." When we come across this marking, it is best to pause and read the section again, slowly and thoughtfully. The next three verses (vv. 6–8) look ahead to the future. They are actually directed to anyone who may read these words. Finally (vv. 9–11), he exhorts the readers to live in an upright manner.

    I. Expression of Present Joy (vv. 1–2)
      "How blessed is he . . . how blessed is the man. . . ."

II. Reflection on Past Sins (vv. 3–5)
   A. Reluctance to confess (vv. 3–4)
   B. Willingness to confess (v. 5)
III. Provision for Future Needs (vv. 6–8)
   A. Invitation (v. 6)
   B. Protection (v. 7)
   C. Guidance (v. 8)
IV. Application to Every Believer (vv. 9–11)
   A. Don't be stubborn! (v. 9)
   B. Take your choice! (v. 10)
   C. Remain upright! (v. 11)

EXPRESSION OF PRESENT JOY

How blessed is he whose transgression is forgiven,
Whose sin is covered!
How blessed is the man to whom the Lord does not impute
   iniquity,
And in whose spirit there is no deceit! [vv. 1–2]

In these two verses David is overjoyed . . . unrestrained and exuberant in his expressions of gratitude to God. The two sentences begin just like Psalm 1 (in Hebrew, that is): "Oh, the happiness many times over!" The idea is that of multiplied, numberless blessings. He is rejoicing over the removal of sins that once pinned him to the mat.

If you look closely, you'll find *four specific terms* for wrongdoing in the first two verses. They describe the downward steps that lead a man to the same condition in which David lived before he finally confessed his wrong.

1. Transgression. The word is from the Hebrew term *phahshaa* meaning "to rebel, revolt." It describes a willful act of disobedience.

2. Sin. This word is from the most common Hebrew term for wrongdoing—*chah-tah:* "to miss the mark, to miss the way, go wrong." It has to do with deviating from the path which pleases God.

3. <u>Iniquity</u>. This term from the Hebrew *ah-wah* goes deeply into our experience after sin has occurred. It means "guilt, punishment of iniquity."

4. <u>Deceit</u>. *Re-mee-ah* is the original Hebrew term, meaning "treachery, deception (and in some cases—as here), self-deception."

Clearly, the songwriter traces the downward spiral of wrong-doing. It is a notorious tailspin with which most of us are familiar. First, we rebel or revolt against God's revealed will. Next, we miss the way He marked out for us—the path of righteousness. Then, guilt grabs us and we go through the inner torment of severe uncomfortable feelings. Without relief, the daily grind of an unforgiven conscience can drive a person mad.

During Billy Graham's crusade in England many years ago, a London psychiatrist told the evangelist that, in his opinion, 70 percent of those in mental institutions could be released immediately if they could find forgiveness—release from their tormenting guilt!

Finally, self-deception sets in, as it did in David when he refused to deal with his wrong. And it can do the same in us.

I remember the words of F. B. Meyer when he wrote concerning a great biblical character's compromise with sin: "No man suddenly becomes base."

Because it happens slowly, many try to tolerate sin's consequences—those inner churnings and grinding turmoil. (We'll look at the daily grind of inner turmoil next week.) If you have fallen into the torments of a guilty conscience through sin and you realize that self-deception is beginning to take over . . . I urge you to stop. Stop your downward plunge and confess your wrong to your Lord. Go to whatever length is necessary to clean up the whole mess. Read these next two statements from Scripture with great care:

> He who conceals his transgressions will not prosper,
> But he who confesses and forsakes them will find compassion.
>   [Prov. 28:13]

> If we confess our sins, He is faithful and righteous to forgive us our sins and to cleanse us from all unrighteousness. [1 John 1:9]

REFLECTION ON PAST SINS

When I kept silent about my sin, my body wasted away
Through my groaning all day long.
For day and night Thy hand was heavy upon me;
My vitality was drained away as with the fever-heat of
    summer.   [Selah.

I acknowledged my sin to Thee, and my iniquity I did not hide;
I said, "I will confess my transgressions to the Lord";
And Thou didst forgive the guilt of my sin.   [Selah.
[v. 3–5]

David takes us back to those tragic days when he refused to acknowledge his wrong (vv. 3–4). These are amazing lyrics in a song that describes what went on inside himself during his tormenting days of unconfessed sin.

He admits when he "kept silent" regarding his sin, he paid a bitter price. The inner conflict brought about what is known as psychosomatic illness . . . the presence of actual physical pain resulting from mental or emotional conflicts—in this case, the refusal to deal completely and honestly with sin. What happened?

—His "body wasted away."
—He groaned "all day long."
—He endured this "day and night."
—His "vitality [literally 'sap, juices'] drained away."
—He had a "fever-heat" like the hot summer.

Abruptly, he adds *Selah*—pause and consider!

Obviously, God's hand was heavy upon him. In the words of Proverbs 13:15: "The way . . . [was] hard." Like a tree trying to survive without water from refreshing rains, David was utterly miserable in this sinful state.

The Modern Language Bible (MLB), a revision of the Berkeley Version in Modern English, renders Proverbs 14:30 as follows: "A relaxed mind makes for physical health, but passion is bitterness to the bones."

Finally, David confessed (Ps. 32:5). Without restraint he poured out his sinful condition. Don't miss the progression:

> Thou didst forgive
> the guilt of my sin.
> [Selah!
>
> I will confess
> my transgressions.
>
> My iniquity I
> did not hide.
>
> I acknowledged
> my sin.

Like a cool, cleansing shower on a hot, sweaty day, God's forgiveness washed away not only the sins but the tormenting guilt. The Lord went far into the depths of David's inner being and provided that magnificent relief only He can bring: PEACE. God forgave completely because David confessed completely.

If you are harboring some sin—if you are keeping hidden a few secret regions of wrong—don't expect to enjoy freedom from guilt, child of God. There is an unspoken axiom threaded through Scripture: secret sin cannot coexist with inner peace. Peace returns only when our sins are fully confessed and forsaken. Few grinds are more galling than the grind of an unforgiven conscience. It's awful! And few joys are more relieving than having our sins forgiven. It's wonderful!

PROVISION FOR FUTURE NEEDS

Therefore, let everyone who is godly pray to Thee in a time
   when Thou mayest be found;
Surely in a flood of great waters they shall not reach him.
Thou art my hiding place; Thou dost preserve me from trouble;
Thou dost surround me with songs of deliverance.   [Selah.
I will instruct you and teach you in the way which you should go;
I will counsel you with My eye upon you. [vv. 6–8]

Remember, the theme of this psalm is *forgiveness*. David wants to make it clear that he doesn't have a corner on this blessed experience. He therefore issues an invitation to "everyone who is godly." This means "every believer"—every person who knows the Lord, having received Jesus Christ by faith. David urges all God's people to pray—even in the midst of "a flood of great waters" when all seems hopeless. He promises that when this is done, God will provide the same deliverance to us He brought to David.

Verse 7 places full attention on God. He is the One who protects us, preserves us, surrounds us, and even gives us a song. Selah (again, pause and consider)! Long enough has the mistaken concept of God been proclaimed—that He is a peeved Deity, some kind of heavenly brute who delights in whipping and buffeting His creatures. No . . . look again at verse 7. David breaks out into songs of deliverance! "Thou art my hiding place; Thou dost preserve me from trouble; / Thou dost surround me with songs of deliverance. [Selah."

What a comforting picture, especially to those who have been in deep sin and seek forgiveness!

The next statement is God's answer to David's invitation to all God's people. In it the Lord promises His guidance and counsel. Literally, the eighth verse concludes: "I will give counsel, keeping my eyes on you. . . ."

Do you have the feeling that God is gone? That God doesn't care? Trust me today; He *does* care. He cares personally about you (1 Pet. 5:7). He has His eyes on you. He may seem to you to be removed and distant . . . but He is near. Christians love to sing the old hymn "How Firm a Foundation":

> "Fear not, I am with thee, O be not dismayed,
> For I am thy God, I will still give thee aid;
> I'll strengthen thee, help thee, and cause thee to stand,
> Upheld by My gracious, omnipotent hand.

> "When through the deep waters I call thee to go,
> The rivers of sorrow shall not overflow,
> For I will be with thee, thy trials to bless,
> And sanctify to thee thy deepest distress.

"The soul that on Jesus hath leaned for repose,
I will not, I will not desert to his foes;
That soul, though all hell should endeavor to shake,
I'll never, no never, no never forsake!"[11]

It is time for us to start believing what we enjoy singing.

APPLICATION TO EVERY BELIEVER

Do not be as the horse or as the mule which have no
    understanding,
Whose trappings include bit and bridle to hold them in check,
Otherwise they will not come near to you.
Many are the sorrows of the wicked;
But he who trusts in the Lord, lovingkindness shall surround
    him.
Be glad in the Lord and rejoice, you righteous ones,
And shout for joy all you who are upright in heart. [vv. 9–11]

David summarizes all the lessons he wants to leave with us
into three strong statements of exhortation:

First: Don't be stubborn! (v. 9).

When it comes to dealing with sin, don't be like a mule or
any other hardheaded beast! Give in . . . and keep an open
account before the Lord. Don't let wrongdoing build up. Don't
try to maintain a standoff any longer.

Second: Take your choice! (v. 10).

In reading over these concluding words, you'll notice two and
only two paths: the path of the wicked (which brings "many sorrows") and the path of trust (which brings "lovingkindness").
Take your choice (says the songwriter), but remember the in-
evitable outcome.

Third: Remain Upright! (v. 11).

If you're looking for green pastures, you'll find them only in
fellowship with your Lord. So don't be a fool! Remain upright.
Stop the downward plunge into deep, involved sin by maintaining an upright walk.

God is so gracious! He has planned a life for His children

that results in inner peace, outer strength, and optimism. But we are sinful and frequently choose to walk our *own* way. In the words of the prince of the prophets: "All of us like sheep have gone astray, / Each of us has turned to his own way. . . ." (Isa. 53:6).

But again, He is so gracious! Though He prefers that we not sin, He is willing to forgive and stay near us during our recovery period. He will completely forgive and restore us if we will completely repent, that is, confess and seek His cleansing.

EFLECTIONS ON AN UNFORGIVEN CONSCIENCE

1. Everyone has known the misery of living with a guilty conscience. Perhaps it was the result of using harsh angry words, or setting out to make another person miserable, or overlooking a child's needs, or taking something that didn't belong to you, or breaking a promise, or being unfaithful to your spouse. The possibilities are endless. Read verses 3–4 once again. Call to mind a time when you experienced what those words describe. Now read verse 5—what a magnificent relief! Pay special attention to the promise of being freed not only from the sin but from the guilt as well. Think about the difference between the two. Thank God for *both*.

2. According to Psalm 32:7, David portrays the Lord as (1) our "hiding place," as (2) One who preserves us from trouble, and (3) One who surrounds us with "songs of deliverance."

   During the balance of this week, fix your mind on those three comforting concepts. Instead of envisioning your Lord as an angry Judge ready to bring down the gavel, recall the safety of His presence, the security of His preservation, and His peaceful "songs of deliverance."

3. Look at the final verse of David's song. We are instructed—in fact, commanded!—to be glad . . . to rejoice . . . to shout for joy. Do you? Are you a person of contagious joy? If not, ask the Lord to bring back the pleasant spirit of happiness you once had. You have been forgiven! You are safe! Few things communicate that better than a smile that is genuine . . . one that emerges from a clear, forgiven conscience.

BOOK 2

For the choir director.
A Maskil of the sons of Korah.

As the deer pants for the water
brooks,
So my soul pants for Thee, O
God.
My soul thirsts for God, for the living
God;
When shall I come and appear before
God?
My tears have been my food day and
night,
While they say to me all day long,
"Where is your God?"
These things I remember, and I pour out
my soul within me.
For I used to go along with the throng
and lead them in procession to the
house of God,
With the voice of joy and thanksgiving, a
multitude keeping festival.

Why are you in despair, O my soul?
And why have you become disturbed
within me?
Hope in God, for I shall again praise
Him
For the help of His presence.

O my God, my soul is in despair within
me;
Therefore I remember Thee from the land
of the Jordan,
And the peaks of Hermon, from Mount
Mizar.
Deep calls to deep at the sound of Thy
waterfalls;
All Thy breakers and Thy waves have
rolled over me.
The Lord will command His
lovingkindness in the daytime;
And His song will be with me in the
night,

A prayer to the God of my life.

I will say to God my rock, "Why hast
   Thou forgotten me?
Why do I go mourning because of the
   oppression of the enemy?"
As a shattering of my bones, my
   adversaries revile me,
While they say to me all day long,
   "Where is your God?"
Why are you in despair, O my soul?
And why have you become disturbed
   within me?
Hope in God, for I shall yet praise Him,
The help of my countenance, and my
   God.   [42:1–11]

Vindicate me, O God, and plead my case
   against an ungodly nation;
O deliver me from the deceitful and
   unjust man!
For Thou art the God of my strength;
   why hast Thou rejected me?
Why do I go mourning because of the
   oppression of the enemy?

O send out Thy light and Thy truth, let
   them lead me;
Let them bring me to Thy holy hill,
And to Thy dwelling places.
Then I will go to the altar of God,
To God my exceeding joy;
And upon the lyre I shall praise Thee, O
   God, my God.

Why are you in despair, O my soul?
And why are you disturbed within me?
Hope in God, for I shall again praise
   Him,
The help of my countenance, and my
   God.   [43:1–5]

THE GRIND OF INNER TURMOIL

I have a "churning place." It's in my stomach . . . on the upper, left side, just below the rib cage. When disturbing things happen, when troubling words are said, when certain letters that contain ugly words or extremely critical comments are read, the churning starts. Do you have a similar thing happen?

One friend of mine says his spot is in his head, specifically his forehead. Another fellow told me his was at the back of his neck. Most folks I know have a particular region that starts to grind within. Any number of things can trigger this feeling. They are common to all of us:

- Bad news
- Strong fears
- Strained relations
- Car accidents
- Almost running out of gas
- Dental work
- Late-night phone calls
- Earthquakes

I find it rather comforting that God's inspired hymnal does not omit the grind of inner turmoil. Since it is so common, I would think it strange if such a topic were not addressed. But before we uncover a few of the more practical remarks, let's take a look at some background information about Psalms 42 and 43.

Immediately, we are surprised to discover that Psalm 42 occupies first place in *Book* 2. Actually, the ancient psalms fall into five divisions or "books." Take the time to thumb through the entire hymnbook of The Psalms for a moment. Note the breakdown:

Book 1: Psalms 1–41
Book 2: Psalms 42–72
Book 3: Psalms 73–89
Book 4: Psalms 90–106
Book 5: Psalms 107–150

A look at the closing of each book shows that each concluding song ends with "Amen" or some other form of doxology. The last one (Psalm 150) is, in fact, one great doxology climaxing in praise—a fitting conclusion to the entire Book of Psalms.

All sorts of suggestions have been given to explain why these ancient songs are divided into five books. Jewish tradition explains this arrangement as a conscious reflection of the Pentateuch (Genesis through Deuteronomy). A Midrash (a Jewish commentary) from the Talmudic period on Psalm 1 states: ". . . as Moses gave five books of laws to Israel, so David gave five books of Psalms to Israel."

No one knows for sure why the psalms are so divided. But there is something of significant importance when we look at this first song in Book 2. I want to suggest that Psalm 42 and Psalm 43 should be taken together as a unit. Two observations lead me to make that suggestion:

1. Psalm 43 has no superscription. Nothing by way of introduction appears before verse 1. This is the only psalm in Book 2 without a superscription. I believe, therefore, it flows quite naturally from the previous song. (Remember, the chapter breaks, like the punctuation markings, have been added to the text of Scripture in later centuries. God's Word is inspired . . . but not the punctuations or various paragraph breakdowns.)

2. The phrase repeated twice in Psalm 42 also appears in identical form in Psalm 43. Notice 42:5, 11, and 43:5:

> Why are you in despair, O my soul?
> And why have you become disturbed within me?
> Hope in God, for I shall again praise Him. . . .

These three identical phrases lead me to believe that these two songs form a natural unit, revolving around a single theme.

Look next at the superscription before verse 1 in Psalm 42: *"For the choir director. A Maskil of the sons of Korah."* Do you remember what we learned about *Maskil* last week? We found that this Hebrew title meant that the song was designed to give insight and wisdom when dealing with certain situations. In Psalm 32, the situation was the need for forgiveness.

What is the situation here in these two songs? Going back to the thrice-repeated statement mentioned above, we see clearly that the situation is inner despair and disturbance. In other words, these two songs have been preserved to provide the reader with wisdom and insight in handling those "blue days," that age-old grind of inner turmoil.

Let's look closely at the term *despair*. The Hebrew word *shah-kak* means "to crouch, bow down." It is used in Job 38:40 to describe a lion in a crouched position, lying in wait for its prey. This song talks about those days when we feel like curling up in the fetal position and quitting! It talks about how we can conquer those feelings rather than succumb to them. Christians frequently have such feelings, give in to them, and make others miserable as they grind their way through the process. The two songs are designed to help us overcome feelings of inner turmoil rather than "churn" our way through life.

As I mentioned earlier, having those disturbing feelings on occasion is quite normal. We do a real disservice to a new Christian by telling him that it is abnormal or sinful to be disturbed at any time. How unrealistic and unbiblical! David wrote many psalms while he was churning within. Of course, it is not normal for a Christian to linger for months in the pit of depression, but all of us should be transparent enough to admit we have days like that. I am comforted that even Jesus Himself on occasion was inwardly troubled (John 11:33; 12:27; 13:21).

Dr. John Henry Jowett, an outstanding preacher of yesteryear, was honest enough to admit in a letter to a friend:

> I wish you wouldn't think I'm such a saint. You seem to imagine that I have no ups and downs, but just a level and lofty

stretch of spiritual attainment with unbroken joy and equanimity. By no means! I am often perfectly wretched and everything appears most murky. I often feel as though my religious life had only just begun, and that I am in the kindergarten stage. But I can usually trace these miserable seasons to some personal cause, and the first thing to do is to attend to that cause, and get into the sunshine again.[12]

I appreciate such vulnerability. The good news is that these two songs help us know how to "get into the sunshine again."

The songwriter begins his Forty-second Song with the familiar words:

> As the deer pants for the water brooks,
> So my soul pants for Thee, O God.
> My soul thirsts for God, for the living God;
> When shall I come and appear before God? [vv. 1–2]

David longs for God—like a thirsty deer in a barren wilderness longs for a cool stream. He says he "pants" for the Lord. In Psalm 119:131 he expresses a similar thought: "I opened my mouth wide and panted, / For I longed for Thy commandments."

God, who was considered by biblical saints as "the fountain of living waters" (Jer. 2:13; 17:13), was sought by the churning singer. Being a man after God's own heart, David passionately yearned for His presence. "My tears have been my food day and night, / While they say to me all day long, 'Where is your God?'" (v. 3).

In his turmoil David misses that inner assurance of God's presence. God has certainly not forsaken His child, but at low, blue moments all of us could testify that there are times when it seems like He has! What do we do to become reassured? How can God become real again when we are feeling low . . . when we are in the grind of such inner turmoil?

> These things I remember, and I pour out my soul within me.
> For I used to go along with the throng and lead them in
>   procession to the house of God,
> With the voice of joy and thanksgiving, a multitude keeping
>   festival. [v. 4]

A more exact rendering of the beginning of this verse would be: "These things I *will* remember. . . ." or, "These things I *would* remember. . . ." David is talking to himself. Sometimes that is great therapy. He is saying that when he is blue, he will call to remembrance past days of victory when God was very real, very present. He says, in effect, "Those were the days, my friend! Those were days of blessing, joy, and thanksgiving!"

After calling to mind such days, he asks:

> Why are you in despair, O my soul?
> And why have you become disturbed within me?
> Hope in God, for I shall again praise Him
> For the help of His presence. [v. 5]

"Why," he asks, "should I feel sad and blue with memories like that?" He admits that such vivid memories of past victory should really encourage him.

When you are "crouched" in turmoil, it helps to think back to previous victories and call to mind specific things God did for you. Remember the same Lord is your Lord right now.

I remember my first year at Dallas Seminary. Cynthia and I lived in a *un*-air-conditioned apartment on campus. It stayed hot during the early fall of the year. Knowing that summer would surely come, we began to pray for a window air conditioner. In fact, we prayed through the winter and spring months for it. We told no one; we just prayed. Nothing happened for months—zero response. Late that spring we made a trip home to Houston during Easter vacation. Summer was coming—still no air conditioner. Dallas would soon be an oven! Our trip home was unannounced. Except for our family, no one knew we were coming. We had not been home visiting Cynthia's folks for even an hour before the phone rang. On the other end of the line was a man from our home church.

Surprised, he said, "Chuck, is that you?"

I answered, "Yes."

His next words were: "Do you and Cynthia need a window air conditioner? We just installed a new central unit and my wife and I thought you two could use the one we've replaced."

What a great God we have!

Similar things have occurred since that happened, but to this day when I get low and blue regarding needs, I call to mind that marvelous day back in the spring of 1960 when He provided for our specific need.

But let's face it, sometimes that doesn't do the job. We get so low that no memory will jar us loose from our turmoil. In verses 6–8, a second technique is suggested:

> O my God, my soul is in despair within me;
> Therefore, I remember Thee from the land of the Jordan,
> And the peaks of Hermon, from Mount Mizar.
> Deep calls to deep at the sound of Thy waterfalls;
> All Thy breakers and Thy waves have rolled over me.
> The Lord will command His lovingkindness in the daytime;
> And His song will be with me in the night,
> A prayer to the God of my life.

Look at that unusual expression: "Deep calls to deep." The songwriter pictures himself on the peaks of Mount Hermon, looking toward Mount Mizar. In his mind he thinks of those awesome sounds and scenes surrounding him—as "deep calls to deep," as God communicates with nature and the unchanging, immutable relationship is enacted. In this case, the snow melts high upon Mount Hermon's peaks, causing the thunderous waterfalls, the rapids in streams below. All this display reinforces his point: "Deep calls to deep."

That which is "deep" in God communicates to that which is "deep" in nature—and suddenly change occurs. It happens all around us:

The "deep" in God calls to the "deep" in trees in the fall . . . and inevitably their leaves turn to beautiful orange, red, and yellow . . . ultimately, they fall and the tree is again barren.

The "deep" in God calls to the "deep" in the salmon . . . and millions travel back over many miles to spawn.

But wait—the psalmist is not talking about trees and fish . . . but rather about himself! As the breakers and waves of inner turmoil "rolled over me"—You speak to me, Lord! Your "deep" calls unto my "deep," and You remind me of that

unchanging relationship of love and joy that exists between us!
And again David asks in verse 11:

> Why are you in despair, O my soul?
> And why have you become disturbed within me?
> Hope in God, for I shall yet praise Him,
> The help of my countenance, and my God.

APPLICATION

What an application this suggests! Between God and His children, there exists an eternal, immutable relationship. The hymns we sing refer to it:

> O love that wilt not let me go;
> I rest my weary soul in Thee. . . .[13]

and

> Loved with everlasting love,
> Led by grace that love to know;
> Gracious Spirit from above,
> Thou hast taught me it is so!
> Oh, this full and perfect peace!
> Oh, this transport all divine!
> In a love which cannot cease,
> I am His, and He is mine.[14]

The next time the feelings of despair bend you low, let His "deep" call to your "deep" and be reminded of that eternal love relationship that is not subject to change. God's Spirit communicates with our spirit—and encourages us at such times.

There is yet another solution to feeling the "blahs." In Psalm 43:1–2 David is back under attack. People problems were upon him . . . and we all know how devestating *they* can be! After pleading for God to intervene, David prays (Ps. 43:3–4):

> O send out Thy light and Thy truth, let them lead me;
> Let them bring me to Thy holy hill,

And to Thy dwelling places.
Then I will go to the altar of God,
To God my exceeding joy;
And upon the lyre I shall praise Thee, O God, my God.

He asks for two specific things: Thy Light and Thy truth.

He wanted the Lord to give him His Word (truth) and an understanding of it (light). Perhaps he sought for a specific statement from Scripture that would be fitting and appropriate for his situation and, equally important, he sought for insight into it. This would bring joy and praise. When this occurred, he asked again (Ps. 43:5):

> Why are you in despair, O my soul?
> And why are you disturbed within me?
> Hope in God, for I shall again praise Him,
> The help of my countenance, and my God.

Every believer in Jesus Christ must ultimately come to the place where he is going to trust God's Word completely before he can experience consistent victory. His Book is our single source of tangible truth. We try every other crutch—we lean on self . . . on others . . . on feelings . . . on bank accounts . . . on good works . . . on logic and reason . . . on human perspective—and we continually end up with the short straw and churning. God has given His written Word and the promise of His light to all His children. WHEN WILL WE EVER LEARN TO BELIEVE IT AND LIVE IN IT AND USE IT AND CLAIM IT? I often wonder how many of His personal promises to His people exist in His Book unclaimed and ignored.

The grind of inner turmoil will not depart forever . . . but its immobilizing presence can be overcome. I hope these two ancient songs will help make that happen in your life this week.

EFLECTIONS
ON INNER TURMOIL

1. Perhaps you have recently been entertaining a low-grade depression . . . feelings of inner unrest or even despair. We just read where the psalmist asked himself, *"Why are you in despair, O my soul?"* (42:5). It's a good time for you to do that. Ask yourself why? It is a great help to pinpoint the reason(s) behind inner turmoil. Once you put your finger on the nerve, talk to God about it. Request His assistance. Express your desire to Him. Ask for relief.

2. Let's look again at 42:8. *The Living Bible* paraphrases it:

   > Yet day by day the Lord also pours out his steadfast love upon me, and through the night I sing his songs and pray to God who gives me life.

   What a thought! All day long: steadfast love poured out . . . all through the night: songs and prayers. Try that the next time the grind of inner turmoil tries to steal your daytime joy or your night's rest. Remind yourself, "I am the recipient of my Lord's steadfast love," or recall the words of a favorite hymn. It works! I know; I did it last night.

3. Here is a surprise suggestion: Break your predictable mold this next weekend. Do something totally different. Go on a picnic. Or fly a kite . . . or both! If you prefer, take a long walk through the woods or a local park. A change in scenery does wonders for getting rid of inner churnings!

PSALM

*For the choir director.
A Psalm of the sons of Korah, set to Alamoth.
A Song.*

God is our refuge and strength,
A very present help in trouble.
Therefore we will not fear,
though the earth should
change,
And though the mountains slip into the
heart of the sea;
Though its waters roar and foam,
Though the mountains quake at its
swelling pride.   [Selah.

There is a river whose streams make glad
the city of God,
The holy dwelling places of the Most
High.
God is in the midst of her, she will not
be moved;
God will help her when morning dawns.
The nations made an uproar, the
kingdoms tottered;
He raised His voice, the earth melted.

The Lord of hosts is with us;
The God of Jacob is our
   stronghold.   [Selah.

Come, behold the works of the Lord,
Who has wrought desolations in the
   earth.
He makes wars to cease to the end of the
   earth;
He breaks the bow and cuts the spear in
   two;
He burns the chariots with fire.
"Cease striving and know that I am God;
I will be exalted among the nations, I will
   be exalted in the earth."
The Lord of hosts is with us;
The God of Jacob is our
   stronghold.   [Selah.
[46:1–11]

THE GRIND OF PERSONAL WEAKNESS

We deny it. We fake it. We mask it. We try to ignore it. But the truth stubbornly persists—we are *weak* creatures! Being sinful, we fail. Being prone to sickness, we hurt. Being mortal, we ultimately die. Pressure wears on us. Anxiety gives us ulcers. People intimidate us. Criticism offends us. Disease scares us. Death haunts us. This explains why the apostle Paul writes: ". . . we ourselves groan within ourselves, waiting eagerly for our adoption as sons, the redemption of our body" (Rom. 8:23).

How can we continue to grow in this bag of bones, covered with weaknesses too numerous to mention? We need a big dose of Psalm 46. What hope for those struggling through the grind of personal weakness!

A great historic hymn of Protestant Christianity found its origin in Psalm 46. Read verse 1 and see if you can determine which hymn I have in mind: "God is our refuge and strength, / A very present help in trouble."

It is, of course, Martin Luther's immortal "A Mighty Fortress Is Our God." Remember the first stanza?

> A mighty fortress is our God,
> A bulwark never failing;
> Our helper He, amid the flood
> Of mortal ills prevailing. . . .[15]

You may not have noticed that the psalm is to be "set to Alamoth." These words are addressed to the choir director. The word *Alamoth* is derived from *Almah,* a Hebrew term meaning "maiden, young woman." Some say, therefore, that this means the song was to be sung by a choir of women—but the place of worship back in the days of the psalms had no such choir. We are given a hint from a reference in 1 Chronicles 15:20, where we read that harps were to be tuned ". . . to Alamoth." The marginal reference in the New American Standard Bible says: "harps of maidenlike tone." Quite likely, this song was to be played on soprano-like instruments, on highly pitched instruments of music. Perhaps this was to make the psalm unique and easily remembered—much like certain lilting strains of Handel's *Messiah* ("For unto us a child is born" or "O Thou, that tellest good tidings to Zion"). This song was to be perpetually remembered.

As you were reading the lyrics, did you notice anything that is repeated? It is true that verses 7 and 11 are identical . . . but look at the thrice-repeated "Selah." As we have pointed out in our previous weekly studies, this is most likely a musical marking that denotes a pause. In Hebrew poetry it suggests our pausing and thinking about what we have just read before proceeding.

The three pause markings assist us in understanding this song. They are built-in hints the reader should not overlook. As in many of the psalms, verse 1 states the theme, which we might render: "God is an immediate source of help (strength), / When we are in a tight squeeze!"

The term translated "trouble" in most versions of the Bible is from a Hebrew verb meaning "to be restricted, to tie up, to be narrow, cramped." It reminds me of an expression we sometimes use to describe the idea of being in a jam: "between a rock and a hard place." It means to be in a pinch or tight squeeze. The psalmist declares that God is immediately available, instantly present in any situation . . . certainly at those times when we are weak!

In the remaining verses he develops this great theme by

describing three very serious situations and his corresponding reaction to each. Let me explain:

Situation 1:   Nature . . . in upheaval
Reaction: I will not fear (vv. 2–3)
                Selah!

Situation 2:   Jerusalem . . . under attack
Reaction: I will not be moved (vv. 4–7)
                Selah!

Situation 3:   Battlefield . . . after war
Reaction: I will not strive (vv. 8–11)
                Selah!

I WILL NOT FEAR

In the second and third verses the psalmist introduces some of the most terrifying scenes in all of life. Each traumatic situation is introduced with the word "though." Count them . . . four in all:

. . . though the earth should change
. . . though the mountains slip into . . . the sea
. . . though its waters roar and foam
. . . though the mountains quake

The picture is familiar to all who live in Southern California, the great land of mud slides, earthquakes, and tremors! The scene is filled with havoc, the situation is awesome, a wild uproar sweeps across the psalmist's life. He feels weak . . . totally helpless. As the earth beneath him shifts, rolls, and slides, his belongings instantly become insignificant and life seems insecure, but even so the songwriter declares, "I will not fear."

Why? How could anyone in such a threatening situation say that? Back to verse 1 for the answer: Because God, our heavenly Father, is our immediate helper, our immutable, ever-present source of strength, our bridge over troubled waters!

When personal weakness begins to plague us, that is a marvelous reminder. God is our "very present help," *our strength.*
  Selah!

I WILL NOT BE MOVED

The scene changes in verses 4–7:

> There is a river whose streams make glad the city of God,
> The holy dwelling places of the Most High.
> God is in the midst of her, she will not be moved;
> God will help her when morning dawns.
> The nations made an uproar, the kingdoms tottered;
> He raised His voice, the earth melted.
> The Lord of hosts is with us;
> The God of Jacob is our stronghold.   [Selah.

The subject? "The city of God" (v. 4). This is a reference to the Jews' beloved Jerusalem. As you read over these inspired stanzas, you quickly discover that the city is under attack. Nations and kingdoms have risen up against her . . . yet "she will not be moved." The reason is clearly stated in the first part of verse 5: "God is in the midst of her."

And it is ratified in verse 7: "The Lord of hosts is with us; / The God of Jacob is our stronghold."

What is it that gave Jerusalem her safety? Quite simply, it was the indwelling, omnipotent presence of Jehovah God!

Do you remember that account in Mark's Gospel (4:35–41, KJV) of the trip Jesus and His disciples made across the Sea of Galilee? It has been made famous by a song believers sing entitled "Peace, Be Still!" The trip was a stormy one and the disciples greatly feared for their lives. Gripped with thoughts of their own personal weakness, they woke Jesus and questioned how He could sleep at a time like that. After calming the wind and the sea, Jesus rebuked the disciples for their lack of faith. How could they ever sink? Why would they fear? They had God in the boat with them! The boat would never sink as long as God was in it. They should not have been moved, for the

Lord Himself was in their midst. I'd call that a perfect illustration of Psalm 46:5 in action.

Look also at the term *moved* in verse 5. It literally means "to totter or shake." We have the descriptive slang expression "all shook up." I suppose it would fit here in verse 5. Because God is in me, I really have no reason to get "shook up." Do you realize, Christian friend, that from the moment the Lord Jesus Christ became the Lord and Savior of your life, He has been living *in you?* In fact, Christ is called "your life" in Colossians 3:4. Furthermore, the hope of glory is "Christ in you." You, child of God, have the Lord God *within you*. In your midst! Therefore, with Him present, there is no reason to totter. God is not going to totter and shake, nor is His dwelling place. So, the next time you are tempted to panic, call to mind that God is literally in your midst.

Selah!

I WILL NOT STRIVE

The last four verses (vv. 8–11) are nothing short of magnificent. Read them over once again.

> Come, behold the works of the Lord,
> Who has wrought desolations in the earth.
> He makes wars to cease to the end of the earth;
> He breaks the bow and cuts the spear in two;
> He burns the chariots with fire.
> "Cease striving and know that I am God;
> I will be exalted among the nations, I will be exalted in the
>   earth."
> The Lord of hosts is with us;
> The God of Jacob is our stronghold.   [Selah.

The scene has changed to a battlefield. The psalmist invites us to view the mute reminders of war. The terrain is strewn with the litter of a battlefield aftermath. The chariots are overturned, burned, and rusty. Bows, spears, and other destroyed implements of warfare are covered with dust and debris. It is a sight to behold! This imaginary tour reminds us of the scenes after World War II . . . the beaches of Normandy, the cities of Berlin, Hiroshima, London, the islands of Iwo Jima, Okinawa. When you look at the remains, it is a moving experience. Rusty tanks. Sunken boats covered with barnacles. Concrete bunkers. A silence pervades. Quietness is fitting. It is as though our God has said, "That is enough!" God's work is a thorough thing.

At this point (v. 10), the writer commands:

"Cease striving and know that I am God;
I will be exalted among the nations, I will be exalted in the
earth."

Look at the word *cease*. The Hebrew term means "relax, do nothing, be quiet!" And the stem of this verb is the causative stem, suggesting that *you* do it! You stop striving, quit racing around . . . relax. Or to use a common expression, "Don't sweat it!" The point is that God is in full control, so let Him handle your situation. As He does, we are to "cause ourselves to relax!" He will be exalted; He is with us.

So much for the ancient songwriter. How about you? Do you live in strife and panic? Is there a fretful spirit about you? Did you realize that God has designed and reserved a spirit of rest for you? Hebrews 4:9 promises: "There remains therefore a Sabbath rest for the people of God."

Does this mean I slip everything into neutral and do nothing? Hardly. It means I first enter that rest He has provided (Heb. 4:11—please read), and then face the situation without panic or strife. If He wants me involved, He will show me clearly and there will be no doubt. My responsibility, however, is to enter deliberately into His invisible sanctuary of rest . . . to trust Him completely for safety. That is my best preparation for battle—to be armed with His Sabbath rest. It is amazing what that does to stop the grind of personal weakness. Listen to what Proverbs 21:31 says: "The horse is prepared for the day of battle, / But victory belongs to the Lord."

In the final analysis, it is the Lord's job to provide the victory over every one of our weaknesses. He can handle whatever is needed. Our striving will never do it.

Selah!

REFLECTIONS ON PERSONAL WEAKNESS

1. Pause (Selah) and consider this. Are you fearful? Are you trapped in your prison of fears, wrapped tightly and squeezed in by worry and pessimism and agitation? These are the signs of a person preoccupied with his or her own weaknesses. God longs to prove Himself as your source of victory, power, and stability. Let me give you some "victory verses." Please read each one.

Genesis 15:1	Hebrews 13:5–6
Joshua 1:9	2 Timothy 1:7
Proverbs 3:5–6	1 Corinthians 15:57–58
Isaiah 40:31; 41:10	Ephesians 6:10–18
Psalm 27:1; 91:1–2, 5–10	1 Peter 5:6–8
Matthew 11:28–30	

   Take your fears, wrap them into a neat mental bundle, and toss them out the window as you read those verses, one by one. Ask the Lord to take each specific fear and replace it with His calm, victorious presence.

2. Find a hymnal and read each stanza of Martin Luther's "A Mighty Fortress Is Our God." Meditate on the vivid word pictures he uses. Hum it to yourself each time you shower this week.

3. Most of us—though weak—continue to strive, don't we? We "sweat the small stuff." We say we're not going to but

we do! This is the week to start breaking that habit. Take the next eight words, "Cease striving and know that I am God," and (1) commit them to memory, (2) say them to yourself each morning this week before you roll out of bed, (3) share them with at least one other person each day this week, and (4) every time you feel the sparks flying off the daily grind of some weakness in your life, say them aloud . . . quietly but aloud. Ask the Lord to take charge as you relax. And I mean really relax.

Selah!

For the choir director; on stringed instruments.
A Maskil of David, when the Ziphites
came and said to Saul,
"Is not David hiding himself among us?"

Save me, O God, by Thy name,
And vindicate me by Thy power.
Hear my prayer, O God;
Give ear to the words of my
mouth.
For strangers have risen against me,
And violent men have sought my life;
They have not set God before
them.   [Selah.

Behold, God is my helper;
The Lord is the sustainer of my soul.
He will recompense the evil to my foes;
Destroy them in Thy faithfulness.

Willingly I will sacrifice to Thee;
I will give thanks to Thy name, O Lord,
for it is good.
For He has delivered me from all trouble;
And my eye has looked with satisfaction
upon my enemies.   [54:1–7]

THE GRIND OF DIFFICULT PEOPLE

The cartoon scene created by Charles Schulz is familiar to most American homes. Charlie Brown and Lucy are engaged in conversation. Lucy's back is turned, her arms are folded and a look of disgust appears on her face. Charlie is pleading, as usual, for her to be tolerant and understanding. With outstretched arms he says:

"Lucy, you *must* be loving. This world really needs love. You have to let yourself love to make this world a better place in which to live!"

Lucy whirls around and screams (as Charlie does his famous back flip):

"Look, blockhead—the *world* I love. It's *people* I can't stand!"[16]

We smile, not because it is an unrealistic cartoon but because it is so very true. There are no problems quite like *people problems*, are there? You can have a job that demands long hours and great physical effort, but neither the hours nor the energy drain gives you the problems difficult people do. You can have financial difficulties, physical pain, a tight schedule, and miles of driving, but these things are not the cause of our major battles. It's *people*, as Lucy said. The grind of difficult people is quite an assignment!

The song we're looking at this week talks about living beyond people problems. It gives us some very practical advice on how to respond to *people* anxieties, problems brought into our lives because of other members of the human race who are just as ornery as we are!

BACKGROUND

If you will take a moment to look at the superscription, you'll find it worth your while. By the way, I hope you are learning to do that when studying the ancient songs in the Bible. The words that appear before the first verse of each psalm are part of the original text, giving the reader some helpful hints about the song. Most folks don't realize that.

In the Fifty-fourth Psalm the superscription reads:

> *For the choir director; on stringed instruments. A Maskil of David, when the Ziphites came and said to Saul, "Is not David hiding himself among us?"*

This is a very lengthy and helpful superscription. From it we learn that David wrote the song. We also learn that it is a *Maskil.* By now we should be getting familiar with the term. We've seen it at other times in our previous weeks' studies. It means "instruction, insight." All Maskil songs are designed to give instruction and insight when dealing with certain situations. In this case, the situation is problems with people, as we've already stated, so we don't have to guess and wonder what prompted David to write it. The historical setting appears here at the beginning . . . an event that is recorded in 1 Samuel 23:14–26.

David is being hunted by jealous King Saul. The singer's hiding place is bleak and rugged. His life is in danger, so he tries to find a place of safety. Everything backfires. He gets to a spot called the *hill of Hachilah* and thinks he is safe. It is Ziphite territory, and so far as he can tell, he has found neutral ground, a place to rest and sleep. But no rest is possible. The Ziphites turn against him and report his whereabouts to Saul. The chase is on again! David then goes to *the wilderness of Maon* but finds himself surrounded by Ziphites and Saul's soldiers. I can just picture David. He is dirty, sweaty, hungry, thirsty, exhausted, and no doubt discouraged. He slumps down beside a leafy bush or beneath the shadow of a rock to escape the searing rays of that Palestinian sun, and he begins to write his feelings in poetic form. He has been attacked and let down by people. Now he is led by the Holy Spirit to record his feelings. Those expressions are what we have today preserved in the lyrics of this song, Psalm 54.

The first three verses are a prayer with emphasis on the enemy. The spotlight then turns to the defender as the next two verses form a picture. The last two verses are words of praise as the defended, David himself, becomes the subject of interest.

THE ENEMY—A PRAYER

> Save me, O God, by Thy name,
> And vindicate me by Thy power.
> Hear my prayer, O God;
> Give ear to the words of my mouth.
> For strangers have risen against me,
> And violent men have sought my life;
> They have not set God before them.   [Selah.
> [vv. 1–3]

Verses 1 and 2 in the Hebrew Bible begin differently than in our English version. Literally, they read: "O God, save me . . . vindicate me. . . ! O God, hear my prayer. . . !"

Normally, the verb appears first in the Hebrew sentence, but in this case it is, "O God . . . O God. . . ." By rearranging the normal word order, great emphasis is placed on God. The emphasis is strengthened by the repetition of His name, "O God . . . O God!"

What we discover immediately is that David gives us a perfect example of what to do when we find ourselves under attack by people. Pray first! Don't wait! Ask for His strength and stability! Normally, we pray last, don't we?

We usually fight back first. We retaliate or develop a resentment for the one who makes life miserable for us.

I read some time ago of an animal, a gnu. It has a curious habit when it is being hunted or when it is cornered. It kneels on it forelegs and remains completely silent, as if in prayer. David was a human gnu and so we should be!

Observe that David requests deliverance and vindication on the basis of two things: God's name and God's power.

> Save me, O God, by Thy name,
> And vindicate me by Thy power.
> Hear my prayer, O God;
> Give ear to the words of my mouth.

Throughout the Old Testament God is called at least twelve different names. Each name signifies a particular aspect of His character. David called to mind God's attributes. He also called upon His power, His omnipotence. We all know our need for strength when people have disappointed us, don't we? God's presence and God's strength are two things we cannot do without when enduring people-related conflicts.

In verse 3, David specifies his problem:

> For strangers have risen against me,
> And violent men have sought my life;
> They have not set God before them.   [Selah.

The enemies are given two descriptive names: "strangers" and "violent men." The first name refers to the Ziphites. The other no doubt refers to Saul and his soldiers.

The term *strangers* comes from a term that means "to scatter, disperse" and is used in the Old Testament for investigating a matter, searching out or tracing something—like spies would do. The Ziphites had become spies for Saul. They were dispersed throughout the land, searching for David.

I mention this because I may be writing to someone as innocent as David was, but perhaps you, too, are being "spied upon;" you're being investigated. It is a frightening thing to be falsely accused, especially when the accusations lead to suspicious actions against you. And it is worse when the enemy is one whom you once trusted as your friend! Like Judas, who turned against the Savior, one who was your friend may have now turned against you. If so, you have One who fully understands your experiences. In fact, He sympathizes with your feelings.

> Since then we have a great high priest who has passed through the heavens, Jesus the Son of God, let us hold fast our confession. For we do not have a high priest who cannot sympathize with our weaknesses, but one who has been tempted in all things as we are, yet without sin. Let us therefore draw near with confidence to the throne of grace, that we may receive mercy and may find grace to help in time of need. [Heb. 4:14–16]

David states that they did not have God set before them. God was not in their thinking. He was not the One responsible for their actions. Their insidious suspicions were not prompted by the Lord, which brings up a very practical point. When people turn against you and you are in the right, it is somewhat like being kicked by a mule; it's best to consider the source! You were kicked by a creature whose nature it is to kick. "Why do the heathen rage?" asks the psalmist. A simple answer could be because *they're heathen!* So, when you're wrongly treated, consider the source. They have not set the Lord before them. He doesn't energize their actions. That means, by the way, that He is on your side, not theirs; so (as we learned in Psalm 46) *relax!*

Before moving on, notice that verse 3 concludes with *Selah,* that musical sign meaning "pause." Do that right now; pause and consider your life for a moment. Think through these verses by making them personal to you.

THE DEFENDER—PICTURE

> Behold, God is my helper;
> The Lord is the sustainer of my soul.
> He will recompense the evil to my foes;
> Destroy them in Thy faithfulness. [vv. 4–5]

The first part of these verses sounds like Psalm 46:1, where we are told that God is ". . . a very present help in trouble." An archaic English term for help is *succor.* It means "to furnish relief." Our Defender does just that. The passage goes on to say He is our "sustainer." He comprises in Himself the highest degree or class of helpers. David says, "If I were to call together all who have helped me, underneath would be the sustaining arms of my Lord." Moses mentioned this same thought in Deuteronomy 33:27:

> The eternal God is a dwelling place,
> And underneath are the everlasting arms;
> And He drove out the enemy from before you,
> And said, "Destroy!"

The fifth verse promises the evil that is planned against David would return upon those who planned it. Their wrong would backfire and God would see to it that David's integrity would win the day.

To picture this, it would help if you would call to mind "The Roadrunner," a familiar Saturday TV cartoon for children (and a host of adults!). The entire program revolves around a victorious roadrunner and a frustrated coyote who tries in vain to capture or kill that speedy little bird. Every ingenious plan backfires against the coyote as the roadrunner inevitably enjoys the last laugh! Without exception, the evil planned against the roadrunner ultimately returns to the coyote.

So it is with the *believer* who maintains his integrity while under the attack of difficult people! The evil planned against us will return upon the attacker, thanks to our Defender! Thanks to His faithfulness, the attack will be foiled. Psalm 91:5–10 (TEV) expresses this same idea:

> You need not fear any dangers at night
> or sudden attacks during the day
> or the plagues that strike in the dark
> or the evils that kill in daylight.
>
> A thousand may fall dead beside you,
> ten thousand all around you,
> but you will not be harmed.

You will look and see
    how the wicked are punished.

You have made the Lord your defender,
    the Most High your protector,
and so no disaster will strike you,
    no violence will come near your home.

We'll look into that song in much greater depth in the second volume of this book.

As I first read verse 5 of Psalm 54, it seemed awfully severe. *Surely it doesn't mean what it says*, I thought. *Surely God won't actually destroy the enemy*, I said to myself. How wrong I was! I looked up the term *destroy* in the Hebrew text. Do you know what it actually means? It is taken from the Hebrew verb *tzah-math*, which means "to exterminate"! In fact, the verb appears in this verse in the *hiphil* stem (causative stem) meaning, literally, "to cause to annihilate"! What I am pointing out is that David is actually declaring, by faith, that God will cause those who have become his enemies to be totally, completely, thoroughly removed! But I remind you that David doesn't do the removing; *God* does.

It is so easy, under pressure, to play God, isn't it? We have thought about the temptation to take our own vengeance before. Romans 12:17–19 warns us against doing that:

Never pay back evil for evil to anyone. Respect what is right in the sight of all men. If possible, so far as it depends on you, be at peace with all men. Never take your own revenge, beloved, but leave room for the wrath of God, for it is written, "Vengeance is Mine, I will repay," says the Lord.

Living beyond the daily grind of difficult people requires our leaving the vengeance to the One who can handle it best.

THE DEFENDER—PRAISE

The attention shifts again. It is now on the psalmist himself. "Willingly I will sacrifice to Thee; / I will give thanks to Thy name, O Lord, for it is good" (Ps. 54:6).

A major step in dealing with difficult people is taken when we can say, "Thank you, Lord, for this painful experience of being misused, misunderstood, and spied upon." David finally reached this point. He not only gave thanks, but he said, "It is good." Something marvelous suddenly happened.

Let me point out what I think took place between verses 6 and 7. I want you to read 1 Samuel 23:26–29 right now.

And Saul went on one side of the mountain, and David and his men on the other side of the mountain; and David was hurrying to get away from Saul, for Saul and his men were surrounding David and his men to seize them. But a messenger came to Saul, saying, "Hurry and come, for the Philistines have made a raid on the land." So Saul returned from pursuing David, and went to meet the Philistines; therefore they called that place the Rock of Escape. And David went up from there and stayed in the strongholds of Engedi.

Do you see? *The enemy actually left.* Suddenly, perhaps as soon as David said, "I will give thanks to Thy name, O Lord, for it is good," the enemy retreated. Then David said: "For He has delivered me from all trouble; / And my eye has looked with satisfaction upon my enemies" (Ps. 54:7).

The enemy had actually turned back, removing the threat of immediate danger. Furthermore, David said his eye could now "look upon my enemies." This is a beautiful expression that describes a man without bitterness. He could look his enemy squarely in the eye.

By the way, that is a fairly good way to tell whom you consider your enemies to be—those you cannot look at eyeball-to-eyeball. If you hold hard resentment, unforgiveness, and hatred for someone, you will find it nearly impossible to look directly into his eyes for a sustained period of time. Haven't you heard the expression, "She dislikes me so much, she won't even *look* at me anymore."

David found no place in his heart for bitterness toward his enemies. That is the way it ought to be. When that is true, our *people problems* have a way of diminishing!

CONCLUSION

I read a little poem many years ago that sounds amusing but isn't so funny when we experience it:

> To dwell above with saints we love,
>   Oh, that will be glory!
> But to dwell below with saints we know,
>   Well . . . that's another story!

It seems strange to me that we all talk of the glory and delight of heaven where we will be surrounded by the very saints we couldn't look at or get along with on earth! Let me urge you to set your house in order, especially the room where you spend time with people. Review this Fifty-fourth Psalm frequently until its principles become second nature to you.

Let's declare war on those ugly habits we cultivate against others—negative feelings, unforgiveness, resentment, competitiveness, grudges, jealousy, revenge, hatred, retaliation, gossip, criticism, and suspicion. Let's leave this rugged, well-worn road forever!

The only other route to take is *love.* The longer I live and the more time I spend with the Lord (and with others), the more I am driven back to the answer to most people's problems: sincere, Spirit-empowered, undeserved love.

How beautifully Amy Carmichael reminds us of this in her small but penetrating book *If.*

> If I belittle those whom I am called to serve, talk of their weak points in contrast perhaps with what I think of as my strong points; if I adopt a superior attitude, forgetting "Who made thee to differ? and what hast thou that thou hast not received?" then I know nothing of Calvary love. . . . [p. 13]

> If I take offense easily, if I am content to continue in a cool unfriendliness, though friendship be possible, then I know nothing of Calvary love. . . . [p. 44]

> If I feel bitterly towards those who condemn me, as it seems to me, unjustly, forgetting that if they knew me as I know myself they would condemn me much more, then I know nothing of Calvary love. [p. 47][17]

REFLECTIONS ON DIFFICULT PEOPLE

1. Difficult people constitute a big slice of everyone's life, don't they? If we allow it to happen, they will dominate our thinking and drain our energy. This week is an excellent time to stop all that nonsense! Right now, make a mental list of those who give you grief. One by one . . . pray. Pray for relief from the grind of their presence. Pray that God will change their hearts (remember, *you* can't). And pray that you will see the day when enmity is replaced with amity. Pray all this week for those three things.

2. In the song we just looked at, we saw the Lord as "my helper" and also "the sustainer of my soul" (v. 4). I suggested the word "Defender." Look up these three words in the dictionary and write the definition of each:

   Helper: _____

   Sustainer: _____

   Defender: _____

   Starting to feel a little more relieved?

3. Here is a gutsy idea. I hope you are game for it. This week, with the right motive, do something thoughtful for someone who has made life difficult for you. Yes, you read that correctly. You may want to write a brief note or send some flowers. <u>Decide on some way to demonstrate love . . . then *do* it.</u> Whatever, extend the love of God and watch Him work!

Now that we have reached the end of the first thirteen weeks of our year together, it is a good time to change gears. I hope the next section will help relieve even more of the grind!

We are one-fourth of our way through the year, a natural turning point and a good place to switch our emphasis from the songs of Scripture to some of the sayings.

For many years I have taught that the Psalms give us a vertical perspective and the Proverbs a horizontal one. The Psalms help us know how to relate to our God, while the Proverbs help us know how to relate to our fellow human beings. The Psalms assist us in our praise and adoration of the Lord. The Proverbs offer us counsel and wisdom in dealing with other people. We need them both in order to maintain our balance.

So then . . . for the next thirteen weeks, let's focus on some of the insightful words Solomon wrote centuries ago. To this day they remain as true as they are timeless. If you're like me, you'll have a tough time deciding which you appreciate the most!

THE SAYINGS IN SCRIPTURE

WEEK 14 THROUGH WEEK 26

PROVERBS

The proverbs of Solomon the son
of David, king of Israel:
To know wisdom and instruction,
To discern the sayings of
understanding,
To receive instruction in wise behavior,
Righteousness, justice and equity;
To give prudence to the naive,
To the youth knowledge and discretion,
A wise man will hear and increase in
learning,
And a man of understanding will acquire
wise counsel,
To understand a proverb and a figure,
The words of the wise and their riddles.

The fear of the Lord is the beginning of
knowledge;
Fools despise wisdom and instruction.

Hear, my son, your father's instruction,
And do not forsake your mother's
teaching;
Indeed, they are a graceful wreath to
your head,
And ornaments about your neck.   [1:1–9]

THE GRIND OF
HUMAN
VIEWPOINT

Every waking moment of our lives we operate from one of two viewpoints: human or divine. I sometimes refer to these as horizontal perspective and vertical perspective. The more popular of the two is human. We much prefer to think, maintain our attitudes, and conduct our lives independently. Human opinions influence us more than God's commands and principles. Horizontal solutions give us greater security and pleasure, unfortunately, than vertical ones. For example, when under the gun of some deadline, we much prefer a tangible way out than God's telling us to trust Him to see us through. Rather than waiting on our Lord to solve our dilemma in His own time, we would normally choose the option of stepping in and manipulating a fast, painless escape.

Because the Book of Proverbs is full of divine wisdom, yet packed with practical counsel, we can anticipate vertical perspective (even though the grind of human viewpoint comes so naturally). The good news is this: The more we pore over the sayings in Scripture, the more oil we will apply to the daily grind of our horizontal perspective. But before I say more about that, let's get a good grasp on the Book of Proverbs as a whole.

Without a doubt, Solomon's sayings offer the most practical, down-to-earth instruction in all the Bible. The entire book of thirty-one chapters is filled with capsules of truth . . . short, pithy maxims that help us face and, in fact, live beyond life's daily grinds. These sayings convey specific truth in such a pointed, easily understood manner, we have little difficulty grasping the message.

The most commonly employed style of expression in Proverbs is the "couplet" . . . two ideas placed next to each other. Take Proverbs 13:10 for example:

> Through presumption comes nothing but strife,
> But with those who receive counsel is wisdom.

Interestingly, in Proverbs there are three main categories of couplets: contrastive, completive, and comparative.

In the contrastive couplet, the key term is usually *but.* One statement is set in contrast to the other statement, and *but* links the statements together; however, it separates the two ideas.

> A wise son accepts his father's discipline,
> But a scoffer does not listen to rebuke. [13:1]

> Poverty and shame will come to him who neglects discipline,
> But he who regards reproof will be honored. [13:18]

> He who spares his rod hates his son,
> But he who loves him disciplines him diligently. [13:24]

In the completive couplets, the second statement completes the first. In these couplets, the key connecting links are usually *and* or *so.*

> The heart knows its own bitterness,
> And a stranger does not share its joy. [14:10]

> Even in laughter the heart may be in pain,
> And the end of joy may be grief. [14:13]

> Commit your works to the Lord,
> And your plans will be established. [16:3]

In the comparative couplets, the one statement serves as a comparison of the other. In such cases, the keys to look for are *"better . . . than"* and *"as . . . so"* or *"like . . . so."*

> Better is a little with the fear of the Lord,
> Than great treasure and turmoil with it. [15:16]

> It is better to live in a corner of the roof
> Than in a house shared with a contentious woman. [25:24]

Very picturesque. Often the comparative sayings are the most graphic.

While we are getting better acquainted with the ancient sayings, I should mention that this is a book full of various kinds of people. Years ago I did an in-depth analysis of Proverbs and was surprised to discover that the book includes over 180 types of people. No wonder it is so helpful when it comes to giving wise counsel for our horizontal living!

The major question is this: Why has God preserved these sayings down through the centuries? If we go back to the opening words of the book, we'll find the answer to that question. You might want to glance back over Proverbs 1:1–9.

As I read those words, I find five reasons God gave us this book of wisdom:

1. To give reverence and obedience to the heart. "The proverbs of Solomon the son of David, king of Israel: To know wisdom and instruction" (1:1–2).

These sayings bring God into proper focus. They help us look at life from God's point of view. They assist us in knowing how to "read" God's reproofs. The Proverbs will help make our hearts obedient.

2. To provide discernment to the eye. "To discern the sayings of understanding" (1:2).

Discern is a crucial term. It means (in the original Hebrew verb) "to separate, to make distinct." The whole idea of giving insight is in Solomon's mind. Proverbs provides us with the ability to distinguish truth from error.

3. To develop alertness in the walk. "To receive instruction in wise behavior, / Righteousness, justice and equity" (1:3).

The original term translated receive carries with it the thought of mobility . . . taking something along with you, carrying something. In this case, what the student of God's sayings carries with him (or her) is "instruction in wise behavior." We glean from the proverbs an alertness in our daily walk. The sayings assist us when we are on the move. They help us "keep on truckin'!"

4. To establish discretion and purpose in life. "To give prudence to the naive, / To the youth knowledge and discretion" (1:4).

Isn't it interesting that the dual objects of verse 4 are the naive and the young? Those who are wide open to everything, who have little knowledge of danger—those who are gullible. Solomon assures us that these sayings will add substance and purpose to our lives.

For all those who wander aimlessly, lacking purpose and embracing merely a human viewpoint of existence, there is hope!

5. To cultivate keenness of mind. "To understand a proverb and a figure, / The words of the wise and their riddles" (1:6).

Finally, these sayings will help us think keenly; they will sharpen the edges of our minds. They will quicken our thoughts and enable us to understand more of life's riddles. And as that occurs, the grind of human viewpoint will slowly be replaced with the wisdom of divine perspective.

EFLECTIONS ON HUMAN VIEWPOINT

1. It is quite possible that you have begun to endure the grind of life strictly from its human perspective: Two-dimensional. Little depth. Less and less hope. That viewpoint comes from a society that leaves God out. Everything is gauged from what can be seen, weighed, measured, and proven. We are learning that God's Book offers a broader, deeper, richer perspective. These sayings in Proverbs have the ability to change your whole outlook. Are you willing? Before going one page further, tell the Lord that you long to have *His* viewpoint . . . that you want *His* wisdom.

2. Maybe you are among the naive. You have perhaps suffered the consequences of being gullible. Look again at Proverbs 1:7. Define "fear of the Lord." What does it mean when it says that such a fear is the beginning of knowledge? Growing up is a painful, slow process . . . but it can happen. It will help you to keep a journal of the things God is teaching you these days. Start one.

3. Tell a friend about your renewed interest in Proverbs. Explain why these sayings can be of help to people. Take along this book and read the five reasons we have the Proverbs available. Ask him (or her) to pray for you as you search for greater wisdom.

Wisdom shouts in the street,
She lifts her voice in the
square;
At the head of the noisy
streets she cries out;
At the entrance of the gates in the city,
she utters her sayings:
"How long, O naive ones, will you love
simplicity?
And scoffers delight themselves in
scoffing,
And fools hate knowledge?
"Turn to my reproof,
Behold, I will pour out my spirit on you;
I will make my words known to you.
Because I called, and you refused;
I stretched out my hand, and no one paid
attention;
And you neglected all my counsel,
And did not want my reproof;
I will even laugh at your calamity;
I will mock when your dread comes,
When your dread comes like a storm,
And your calamity comes on like a
whirlwind,

When distress and anguish come on you.
"Then they will call on me, but I will not
    answer;
They will seek me diligently, but they
    shall not find me,
Because they hated knowledge,
And did not choose the fear of the Lord.
"They would not accept my counsel,
They spurned all my reproof.
"So they shall eat of the fruit of their own
    way,
And be satiated with their own devices.
"For the waywardness of the naive shall
    kill them,
And the complacency of fools shall
    destroy them.
"But he who listens to me shall live
    securely,
And shall be at ease from the dread of
    evil." [1:20–33]

THE GRIND OF DISOBEDIENCE

Let's face it, we are a pretty wayward flock of sheep! It's not so much that we are ignorant, but rather that we are disobedient. More often than not we know what we ought to do. We just, plainly and simply, do not do it. And so our days are often spent having to endure the irksome and painful consequences of going our own way. The grind of disobedience is neither easy nor new. Unfortunately, it is a well-worn path.

Solomon's sayings address this tendency of ours head-on. The secret of counteracting our bent toward waywardness rests with *wisdom*. In those verses you just read (Prov. 1:20–33), wisdom is personified. She is portrayed as a courageous heroine who stands in the street (symbolic of everyday life) and shouts! She is calling for our attention. She doesn't want us to drift throughout the day without taking her along as our companion. As I read these verses, I observe three facts related to wisdom:

1. Wisdom is available (vv. 20–21).
2. Wisdom can be ignored or spurned (vv. 24–25).
3. Living without wisdom results in serious consequences (vv. 26–28, 31–32).

The deeper we dig into Solomon's sayings, the more clearly we discover what brings wisdom into our lives. The secret? Accepting God's reproofs. Jump ahead for a moment and look at a "completive couplet" with me from Proverbs 3:11–12:

> My son, do not reject the discipline of the Lord,
> Or loathe His reproof,
> For whom the Lord loves He reproves,
> Even as a father, the son in whom he delights.

And while we're at it, look at another even more serious saying in Proverbs 29:1:

> A man who hardens his neck after much reproof
> Will suddenly be broken beyond remedy.

Reproof is from a Hebrew term that means "to correct . . . to convince." I often think of reproofs as God's proddings, those unmistakable nudges, His "still small voice." They are inner promptings designed to correct our ways. They alert us to the fact that we are off course. They communicate, in effect, "My child, that's wrong; change direction!"

These God-given "reproofs" sometimes appear in Scripture. They are spelled out—one, two, three. For example, glance at Proverbs 6:23–24:

> For the commandment is a lamp, and the teaching is light;
> And reproofs for discipline are the way of life,
> To keep you from the evil woman,
> From the smooth tongue of the adulteress.

God's Book shines bright lights into dimly lit caves of immorality, shouting "Danger! Do not enter!" There are dozens of scriptures that offer similar reproofs. Such inner restraints may be silent, but they are nevertheless eloquent.

On other occasions the reproofs come verbally from those who love us. For example:

- From children: "Dad, you're sure gone a lot." Or, "Mom, you seem to be pretty impatient."

- From employers: "You're not showing the same enthusiasm you once did." Or, "You've been coming in late to work recently."

- From friends: "Is something wrong? Your attitude is negative!"

- From a wife: "I feel that you're getting pretty selfish, Hon."

- From a husband: "You don't seem very happy these days. Are you aware that your tone of voice is harsh?"

All of us have sagging character qualities that need attention. To ignore them is to open the gate that leads to disobedience. To address them is to learn and grow from God's personal reproofs. I have listed over thirty character traits in the Reflections section of this week's chapter, specifying some areas worth our attention.

A big question remains: Why? Why do we ignore life's reproofs? What does Solomon say about the reasons we refuse reproofs? As we look back at those sayings in Proverbs 1, I find four reasons reproof is refused. Hold on tight . . . they may hurt!

1. <u>Stubbornness</u>. "Because I called, and you refused . . ." (1:24).

See that last word—*refused?* It means literally "to directly refuse." It is used most often in the Old Testament for refusing established authority, stubbornly and openly rejecting it, as in the case of Pharaoh, who refused to let the Hebrews go. In another of Solomon's sayings, the sluggard *refuses* to get a job. A stubborn will stiff-arms reproofs.

2. <u>Insensitivity</u>. ". . . I stretched out my hand, and no one paid attention" (1:24).

When Solomon states that "no one paid attention," he uses a term that suggests lack of awareness. It would correspond to the New Testament concept of being "dull of hearing." If you have ever tried to pierce through the armor plate of an insensitive individual, you know how frustrating it can be. Though wisdom "stretches out her hand," there are many who completely miss her message due to a lack of awareness.

3. <u>Indifference</u>. "And you neglected all my counsel . . ." (1:25).

To neglect means "to let go." In other words, to keep something from making any difference. This individual says, in effect, "I really couldn't care less!" This is often evidence of low self-esteem. In Proverbs 15:31–32, Solomon writes:

> He whose ear listens to the life-giving reproof
> Will dwell among the wise.
> He who neglects discipline despises himself,
> But he who listens to reproof acquires understanding.

4. <u>Defensiveness.</u> ". . . and did not want my reproof" (1:25).

The Hebrew language is extremely vivid! The original word translated "did not want" means "to be unwilling, unyielding, one who won't consent." This individual is usually defensive and proud.

Disobedience grinds on, most often not because we don't know better but because we don't heed God's reproofs, which are a primary source of wisdom. It's initially more satisfying, quite frankly, to disobey. It can also seem far more exciting and adventurous. But in the long run, every time we fight against wisdom, we lose. A bit of "folk wisdom" comes to mind: "Never git in a spittin' match with a skunk. Even if ya out-spit him, ya come out stinkin'."

Enough said.

REFLECTIONS ON DISOBEDIENCE

1. Take a close look at these character qualities. Circle those that would rank near the top of your personal struggle list.

Alertness	Discernment	Love	Sincerity
Appreciation	Discipline	Loyalty	Submissiveness
Compassion	Efficiency	Objectivity	Tactfulness
Confidentiality	Enthusiasm	Patience	Teachability
Consistency	Flexibility	Peacefulness	Thoroughness
Cooperativeness	Gentleness	Punctuality	Thoughtfulness
Courtesy	Honesty	Self-control	Tolerance
Creativity	Humility	Sense of humor	Understanding
Dependability	Initiative	Sensitivity	Unselfishness

2. God's reproofs don't always come directly from God's Word. He doesn't limit His warnings to specific commands or precepts found in His Book. As we discovered in this chapter, they can come through parents, friends, children, mates, employers, neighbors, a policeman, a teacher, a coach . . . any number of people. And they aren't always verbalized. A look can convey a reproof. All this week, be more sensitive to the reproofs of others.

3. We learned of four reasons most people refuse reproofs. Can you repeat them?

_____   _____

_____   _____

Choose someone you know well enough to be vulnerable with and discuss which of those four reasons represents your most consistent battleground. Probe to find out why. Ask the Lord to help you break the bad habit(s) so you can begin to get a handle on disobedience.

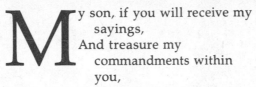

My son, if you will receive my
    sayings,
And treasure my
    commandments within
    you,
Make your ear attentive to wisdom,
Incline your heart to understanding;
For if you cry for discernment,
Lift your voice for understanding;
If you seek her as silver,
And search for her as for hidden
    treasures;
Then you will discern the fear of the
    Lord,
And discover the knowledge of God.
For the Lord gives wisdom;
From His mouth come knowledge and
    understanding.
He stores up sound wisdom for the
    upright;
He is a shield to those who walk in
    integrity,
Guarding the paths of justice,
And He preserves the way of His godly
    ones.
Then you will discern righteousness and
    justice
And equity and every good
    course. [2:1–9]

THE GRIND OF SHALLOWNESS

In our image-conscious, hurry-up lifestyle, hitting the high spots is in vogue—doing just enough to get by. No big deal . . . it's okay to ignore depth in your life so long as you project an image that says you've "got it all together."

Nonsense! People who really make a dent in society are those who peel off the veneer of shallow superficiality and live authentic lives that have depth.

This week, let's level our gun barrels at shallowness. Let's allow the sayings we just read to cut cross-grain against our times and speak with forceful relevance. I should warn you ahead of time, this may not be easy. Solomon takes us into a mine shaft, as it were, a place of hard work, but it will lead us to a most valuable discovery.

As I look closely at these nine verses in Proverbs 2, I find that they can be divided rather neatly into three sections:

   I. The Conditions (vv. 1–4—emphasis on the worker)
      (Note: "if . . . if . . . if . . .")
  II. The Discovery (v. 5—emphasis on the treasure)
      (Note: "then . . .")
 III. The Promises (vv. 6–9—emphasis on the benefits)
      (Note: "For . . .")

Let's dig deeper.

You say you're tired of that daily grind of shallowness?

Weary of faking it? Good for you! But you must remember that breaking out of that mold is awfully hard work. Solomon writes about that when he presents *the conditions* of deepening our lives. "If we will do this . . ." "If we are committed to doing that . . ." Tough talk!

I find four realms of discipline that we must come to terms with if we hope to live beyond the grind of shallowness.

1. The discipline of the written Word of God. "My son, if you will receive my sayings, / And treasure my commandments within you" (v. 1).

It is essential that we receive God's sayings—take them in on a regular basis and allow them to find lodging in our minds. Few things are more astounding in our world than biblical ignorance. People who go beneath the surface of shallow living treasure God's truths and saturate their minds with the Scriptures.

2. The discipline of inner desire. "Make your ear attentive to wisdom, / Incline your heart to understanding" (v. 2).

If we read that correctly, we'll need to have an attentive ear to God's reproofs (remember last week's subject?) and cultivate an open heart before Him.

Are you ready for that? I mean, really motivated? If so, look at the next level.

3. The discipline of prevailing prayer. "For if you cry for discernment, / Lift your voice for understanding" (v. 3).

Perhaps the single most overlooked (and among the most difficult) discipline in the Christian life is consistent prayer. Prevailing prayer. Fervent prayer. In such prayer we "cry for discernment" and we "lift our voice for understanding." In prayer, the sincere believer puts an end to a quick tiptoe trip through the kingdom, chattering like children running through a mall. This person gets down to serious business.

4. The discipline of daily consistency. "If you seek her as silver, / And search for her as for hidden treasures" (v. 4).

We're talking diligence and effort here! The saying describes our seeking God's truths as though digging for silver and searching His mind as we would pursue hidden treasures. This is no superficial game—it's a heavy, consistent pursuit of the living God!

And the results? The discovery?

> Then you will discern the fear of the Lord,
> And discover the knowledge of God. [v. 5]

We'll find true treasure: the fear of the Lord (we'll start taking Him seriously) and the knowledge of God (we'll get to know Him intimately).

Finally, He promises us benefits—benefits from within, without, and above.

1. *From within:* wisdom, knowledge, understanding.

> For the Lord gives wisdom;
> From His mouth come knowledge and understanding. [v. 6]

2. *From without:* protection.

> He stores up sound wisdom for the upright;
> He is a shield to those who walk in integrity,
> Guarding the paths of justice,
> And He preserves the way of His godly one. [vv. 7–8]

3. *From above:* righteousness, justice, equity.

> Then you will discern righteousness and justice
> And equity and every good course. [v. 9]

Yes, "every good course" will accompany the path of those who get rid of shallowness.

Aren't you tired of trifling with sacred things? Haven't you had your fill of superficial skating? Isn't it about time to move off the barren plateau of spiritual neutrality?

This week . . . yes, *this* week, dig in. I dare you!

EFLECTIONS
ON SHALLOWNESS

1. Memorize the first five verses of Proverbs 2 this week. You said you wanted to grow deeper, didn't you? Well, here's a place to start. If you really want to get with it, memorize all *nine* verses.

2. Go back and review the four disciplines taken from Proverbs 2:1–9. Be honest . . . which one represents the biggest challenge for you? Each day this week remind yourself of the discipline, pray about it, search for ways to turn your prayer into action. Think very practically:

   • What are the obstacles?

   • Who stands in your way?

   • Why do you hesitate?

   • What can be done *now?*

3. Focus on "the fear of the Lord" and on "the knowledge of God." Record your own definitions of both:

   Fear: _____

   Knowledge: _____

   Choose a category of your life where "the fear of the Lord" could be applied. Do the same with "the knowledge of God." Be specific. Share the results with your best friend.

My son, do not forget my teaching,
But let your heart keep my commandments;
For length of days and years of life,
And peace they will add to you.
Do not let kindness and truth leave you;
Bind them around your neck,
Write them on the tablet of your heart.
So you will find favor and good repute
In the sight of God and man.
Trust in the Lord with all your heart,
And do not lean on your own understanding.
In all your ways acknowledge Him,
And He will make your paths straight.   [3:1–6]

THE GRIND OF WORRY

This chapter is dedicated to all of you who have worried in the past . . . all of you who are now worried . . . and all who are *making plans to worry soon!* That might sound amusing, but worry is no laughing matter. Quite frankly, it is a sin. It is, however, one of the "acceptable" sins in the Christian life. We would never smile at a Christian who staggered into his home night after night drunk and abusive. But we often smile at a Christian friend who worries. We would not joke about a brother or sister in God's family who stole someone's car, but we regularly joke about our worrying over some detail in life.

Worry is serious business. It can drain our lives of joy day after day. And there is not one of us who doesn't wrestle with the daily grind of it. In the following study we will look at Solomon's answer to this age-old habit unique to humanity.

Instead of focusing on all six verses at the beginning of Proverbs 3, let's spend some time in those last two. They may be familiar to some, but I have the feeling they have more in them than most of us ever realized.

Please glance back and re-read the final two verses of this saying once again. As you do, think about how to rid your life of that all-too-familiar grind of worry.

A primary rule in meaningful Bible study is to determine the context. These verses fall into a surrounding atmosphere of verses that "sets the stage." Let me show you:

1:8 *Hear, my son, your father's instruction* . . .
1:10 *My son* . . .
1:15 *My son* . . .
2:1 *My son* . . .
3:1 *My son* . . .
3:11 *My Son* . . .
3:21 *My son* . . .

Solomon is giving some wise "fatherly advice" to his son in this section of his book. If you should ever take the time to read the first seven chapters, you will discover they are intensely potent and practical. They contain vital information on how to live a stable, wise, well-balanced life. Proverbs 3:5–6, therefore, contains truth for everyday living—the kind of truth that will assist us toward a meaningful life free of worry.

OBSERVATIONS

There are three initial observations I want to make about Proverbs 3:5–6. Then I want to break the verses into smaller parts so that when we put the saying together it makes better sense to you.

1. There are four verbs in these two verses. Verbs are action words and therefore of special interest to all who want to live beyond the daily grind.

- trust
- lean
- acknowledge
- make straight

Three of these terms are *imperatives;* in other words, they are commands. They are directed to the child of God. They are *our* responsibility: *"Trust . . . do not lean . . . acknowledge. . . ."*

The last is the simple declaration of a *promise.* It declares God's part in the verse. It states *His* responsibility: *". . . He will make your paths straight."*

Before going to the next observation, let's understand that these four words give us a very brief outline:

I. <u>My Part</u>
   A. Trust!
   B. Do not lean!
   C. Acknowledge!

II. <u>God's Part</u>
   A. He will make straight. . . .

2. The same term is mentioned four times. Can you find it? Sure, it is the term *your.* Your responsibility in a given situation is to trust with all *your* heart . . . refuse to lean on *your* understanding . . . acknowledge Him in all *your* ways . . . so that He might make straight *your* paths.

3. The first phrase is linked with the last phrase, giving us the main idea. The two in the middle merely amplify the main idea. Let me explain.

The main idea of these verses is, <u>I am to trust in my Lord without reservation—with all my heart—so that He makes my paths straight</u>. What is involved in trusting with all my heart? Two actions: one negative, the other positive.

Negative: *I am not to lean on my own understanding.*
Positive: *I am to acknowledge Him in all my ways.*

CLARIFICATION

Without the desire to be pedantic, I want us to dig into the meaning of several terms. I believe it will help you to understand their original meaning and to see how they fit together. At the end I'll tie up all the loose ends with an amplified paraphrase.

1. Trust. At the root of the original Hebrew term is the idea of throwing oneself down, lying extended on the ground— casting all hopes for the present and the future upon another, finding shelter and security there.

To illustrate this, look at Proverbs 11:28:

> He who trusts in his riches will fall,
> But the righteous will flourish like the green leaf.

We are told *not* to trust in riches, for riches are not secure (see Proverbs 23:4–5). If you set your heart on getting rich, throwing yourself down upon them so as to find your security, you will be sadly disappointed. Riches fail and fade away. Riches do not deserve our trust.

Next, glance at Proverbs 3:21–23:

> My son, let them not depart from your sight;
> Keep sound wisdom and discretion,
> So they will be life to your soul,
> And adornment to your neck.
> Then you will walk in your way securely,
> And your foot will not stumble.

The word translated *securely* is the same Hebrew root word as our term *trust.* We are commanded by our Lord to cast ourselves *completely, fully, absolutely* on Him—and Him only!

2. Lord. This, as you may know, is the most intimate and sacred name for God in all the Bible. To this day Orthodox Jews will not even pronounce it. It is the title given Israel's covenant-keeping God . . . the One who is bound to His people by love and by promise. To us, it is applied to our Lord Jesus Christ, God's precious Son. We are to rely fully upon Him, finding our safety and security in Him. He, *unlike money,* is dependable.

3. Heart. This does not refer to the bodily organ in the chest that pumps blood. It is used throughout the Old Testament to refer to our "inner man," that part of us that constitutes the seat of our intellect, emotion, and will—our conscience and our personality. What is the Lord saying? He is saying we are to cast upon our Savior-God our *total* trust, not holding back in any area of our mind or will or feeling. That, my friend, is quite an assignment!

4. Understanding. I direct your attention to this word next because it appears first in its phrase in the Hebrew Bible.

Literally, the second part of verse 5 says: ". . . and upon your understanding, do not lean." This word *understanding* has reference to *human* understanding. It means that we are not to turn first to our own limited point of view, our own ideas or way of thinking, but to our Lord's wisdom.

5. Lean. This is the Hebrew *shan-ann,* meaning "to support oneself, as though leaning for assistance." It occurs in Judges 16:26 where blind Samson leaned against the huge pillars supporting the Philistine temple. It also appears in 2 Samuel 1:16 where King Saul leaned upon his spear for support. It represents the idea of resting one's weight upon something else as though leaning on a crutch. You will notice the strong negative: ". . . do not lean on your own understanding."

We have a gentleman in our church who could tell you about this much better than I. He was injured on a ski outing several years ago and as a result he was confined to crutches for many long weeks. Sometimes you would find him panting at the top of a flight of stairs. If you looked at his hands, you would notice they had gotten red and sore. The man found that leaning on crutches was *exhausting*.

So is leaning on our own understanding! If you want to spend an exhausting day, try to work out your circumstances leaning on your *human viewpoint*. Chase down all the possibilities you can think of. When you hit a dead-end street, back out, then turn down into another one. Drive fast, then slam on your brakes. Try a dash of panic, a pinch of fear, add a tablespoon of manipulation, three cups of scheming, and a handful of pills! When you are through, consider where you have been. That is an excellent recipe for "instant depression." Furthermore, you will be mentally exhausted. Peace will flee from you.

MAN says: *Why trust when you can worry?*
GOD says: *Why worry when you can trust?*

6. Acknowledge. This means "to recognize." Rather than leaning on the manmade crutch of our own devices, we are exhorted to recognize God's presence and His will in our plight.

By acknowledging Him we remind ourselves that we are not alone.

7. <u>Make straight.</u> The Hebrew term means "to make smooth, straight, right." It includes the idea of removing obstacles that are in the way. It appears in a particular stem (*Piel* stem) that suggests *intensity*. In other words, when the Lord is fully relied upon to handle a given situation, He will remove all the obstacles and smooth out our path thoroughly, not halfheartedly.

APPLICATION

Now that we have analyzed all the vital parts, let's put the verses back together in an extended paraphrase:

> Throw yourself completely upon the Lord—that is, cast all your present and future needs on Him who is your intimate Savior-God . . . finding in Him your security and safety. Do this with all your mind and feeling and will. In order to make this possible, you must refuse to support yourself upon the crutch of human ingenuity. Instead, recognize His presence and concern in each one of your circumstances. Then He (having taken full control of the situation) will smooth out and make straight your paths, removing each obstacle along the way.

From now on when you find yourself approaching the grind of worry, turn to this paraphrase and read it aloud.

REFLECTIONS
ON WORRY

1. Each remaining morning of this week read the paraphrase I have suggested. But instead of reading "that is, cast *all your present and future needs* on Him," insert the specific things that you are tempted to worry about.

2. Locate a pair of crutches. Borrow them from a friend or maybe from a local hospital. Try walking with crutches for an hour each day this week. When you are not on them, carry them in your car or prop them up by the table where you eat and by the bed where you sleep. Why? They will be a tangible, irritating reminder of how bothersome it is to the Lord for you to "support yourself on the crutch of human ingenuity."

3. All this week, think *seriously* about how sinful it is to worry. Yes, call it sin! Realize that it breaks that vital fellowship between you and God. Ponder the fact that when we carry our own burdens we are saying to God "No help needed!" As soon as you get even a fleeting thought to worry, deliberately give it to the Lord. Tell Him that you are refusing to lean any longer on your own abilities.

My son, give attention to my
    words;
  Incline your ear to my
    sayings.
Do not let them depart from your sight;
Keep them in the midst of your heart.
For they are life to those who find them,
And health to all their whole body.
Watch over your heart with all diligence,
For from it flow the springs of
  life. [4:20–23]

THE GRIND OF AN UNGUARDED HEART

At first glance this may seem to be a rather remote area of concern. After all, what is an unguarded heart in comparison to something as real as worry or as troublesome as disobedience? How could anyone struggle that much with an unguarded heart? Well, you may be surprised. To unveil our hearts and put all our secrets on display is to open ourselves to enemy attack. Our Lord is pleased when we reserve an "inner vault" of our lives to hold His treasures. To "tell it all" is to traffic in a world of superficiality. Once we have done a little digging into this subject, I think you will realize how pertinent this daily grind can be.

To begin with, let's remember what I mentioned earlier, that the *heart* in Solomon's sayings is never a reference to the organ in the chest that pumps blood. We learned in last week's reading that it is a term used to describe our whole inner being . . . the center of our mind, our emotions, and our will. In fact, the Hebrew word *labe* is used over ninety times in Proverbs alone.

So when I address an "unguarded heart" this week, I have in mind the very common problem of living without inner restraint, without concern for protection from the adversary, being insensitive to God's delicate leading. Now you see why I feel this is just as great a hassle as the others we've been dealing with . . . maybe greater!

As we look at the saying of Solomon in Proverbs 4, we'll notice we are, again, in one of the "My son . . ." sections. Here is more wise counsel from a father to his family members. Observe his comment about inclining your ear to his sayings and keeping them "in the midst of your heart." Very interesting!

For the next few minutes I want us to direct our full attention to this whole idea of guarding the heart, or, as Solomon put it:

> Watch over your heart with all diligence,
> For from it flow the springs of life. [Prov. 4:23]

I notice three significant observations:

1. This is a command—"Watch over!"

2. There is an intense priority included in this command—"with *all* diligence."

3. The reason for the command is stated in the last part of the verse—"for. . . ."

KEY TERMS

As you may have noticed, there are several words that are keys toward understanding the full meaning of the statement.

Watch over, diligence, and *springs* would have to be understood before the true meaning can emerge. So, now let's dig into each one of them.

1. Rather than beginning the verse as our English version does, the Hebrew text begins with: "More than all else" or "Above all else. . . ."

In Hebrew, when something appears first in a sentence, different from the normal word order, that word is emphatic. That means these words "more than all else" are emphatic. This tells us that our God puts a premium on the matter. Actually, these beginning words are a literal translation of "with all diligence."

We have now established that the verse begins: "More than all else . . ."

2. The next part of the Hebrew verse refers to something that is to be watched closely. Actually, the word originally

comes from a noun which means "a place of confinement." It is periodically rendered *prison,* and in a broader sense it means something that is closely observed, protected, preserved, or guarded.

That gives us even more light. If we went a step further, inserting those thoughts, the verse would read: "More than all else to be closely watched and protected (as something in a confined place). . . ."

3. Now we come to the main Hebrew verb translated *watch over* in English. It is the word *nah-tzaar,* meaning "to preserve, keep." This same word occurs in Isaiah 26:3:

> "The steadfast of mind Thou *wilt keep* in perfect peace,
> Because he trusts in Thee." [Emphasis mine]

The Lord's peace preserves and keeps the believer's mind, making us "steadfast." In Solomon's saying, the words "your heart" follow that same verb:

> More than all else to be closely watched and protected (as something in a confined place), preserve your heart (your inner self, the place where God speaks to you through His Word and Spirit). . . .

We are beginning to understand why this is so essential, why it is imperative for our "heart" to be watched over and preserved, kept sensitive.

4. The word *for* could just as well be rendered *because.* Now we are told *why.*

5. The Hebrew says: ". . . because from within it. . . ." Referring to the heart, the verse declares that it is to be closely protected and kept in a state of "readiness," because it is *within* it that something extremely important occurs.

6. The Hebrew *mo-tzah* is translated "springs," but the word *source* or *direction* would be more accurate. Why is the heart to be protected and kept sensitive to the Lord? ". . . because from within it comes direction for life." Basically, then, we find this verse is dealing with the will of God—both discovering it and walking in it.

ACTUAL MEANING

Now let's put all the pieces of our research together and see what the verse actually says. A paraphrase based on the Hebrew text might read:

> More than all else to be watched over and protected (as something in a confined place), it is imperative that you preserve and keep your heart sensitive; because from within it comes divine direction for your life.

Read that over again, this time very slowly.

The verse is saying that since your inner self—your heart—is the source and basis of knowing God's will, it is more important than *any other single thing* that your heart be in a state of readiness, receptivity, and sensitivity.

If your heart is carnal, calloused, and bent on having your own way, then direction from God for life will not come through. Look at Psalm 16:11:

> Thou wilt make known to me the path of life;
> In Thy presence is fullness of joy;
> In Thy right hand there are pleasures forever.

We learn from that statement that God wants to show His children His plan for their lives.

HOW GOD DIRECTS

Look at Proverbs 4 for one final glance. Go back to the beginning of the chapter. In the first four verses God tells us how He directs us—how He speaks to our "heart."
First, verses 1–4:

Hear, O sons, the instruction of a father,
And give attention that you may gain understanding,
For I give you sound teaching;
Do not abandon my instruction.

When I was a son to my father,
Tender and the only son in the sight of my mother,
Then he taught me and said to me,
"Let your heart hold fast my words;
Keep my commandments and live."

The *Word of our Father* directs us.
Second, verses 5–7:

Acquire wisdom! Acquire understanding!
Do not forget, nor turn away from the words of my mouth.
Do not forsake her, and she will guard you;
Love her, and she will watch over you.
The beginning of wisdom is: Acquire wisdom;
And with all your acquiring, get understanding.

The practical application of our Father's Word to life's decisions helps direct us into His will. This explains why Solomon uses the words "wisdom" and "understanding" several times. The Lord desires for us to apply *practical common sense* in determining His will.
Third, verses 10–11, 20–22:

Hear, my son, and accept my sayings,
And the years of your life will be many.
I have directed you in the way of wisdom;
I have led you in upright paths. . . .

My son, give attention to my words;
Incline your ear to my sayings.
Do not let them depart from your sight;
Keep them in the midst of your heart.
For they are life to those who find them,
And health to all their whole body.

Solomon reminds us of the value of *trustworthy counselors* in these verses. Specifically, he wrote to his own child. He assures his son that the counsel of a godly parent is one of several ways God directs our hearts.
Fourth, verses 26–27:

> Watch the path of your feet,
> And all your ways will be established.
> Do not turn to the right nor to the left;
> Turn your foot from evil.

A final word regarding evaluation always helps. "Watch" means "weigh," as one would weigh baggage. Look discerningly into the matter. *Personal evaluation* (meditation) is another very important part of knowing God's will.

All these things explain why it is important to keep your heart open, sensitive, and carefully watched. Unless it is right before God, He cannot communicate divine direction. And unless we receive and walk in His will, misery and ultimate unhappiness are our constant companions.

Now, let me ask you: Is an "unguarded heart" really that important?

EFLECTIONS ON AN UNGUARDED HEART

1. Let's see how well you understood Solomon's saying in Proverbs 4:23.

   • "Heart" would include the _mind_, _will_, and _emotion_.
   • "Springs" of life means _source_ or _direction_.
   • God wants to show us His will ____ True ____ False?

   Check and see how you did.

2. From Proverbs 4, I presented some ways God directs us into His will:

   • His Word, the Bible
   • Common sense
   • Trustworthy counselors
   • Personal evaluation

   As you look over that list, which has proven the most helpful to you? Why?

3. Think of three ways you could do a better job of "guarding your heart." What has been allowed to slip in that could make it insensitive or slow to react? You may wish to confine your answers to three areas:

   My mind _____.

   My emotions _____.

   My will _____.

Then he taught me and said to me,
"Let your heart hold fast my
words;
Keep my commandments and live;
Acquire wisdom! Acquire
understanding!" [4:4]

My son, observe the commandment of
your father,
And do not forsake the teaching of your
mother;
Bind them continually on your heart;
Tie them around your neck.
When you walk about, they will guide
you;
When you sleep, they will watch over
you;
And when you awake, they will talk to
you.
For the commandment is a lamp, and the
teaching is light;
And reproofs for discipline are the way of
life. [6:20–23]

Keep my commandments and live,
And my teaching as the apple of your eye.
Bind them on your fingers;
Write them on the tablet of your
heart. [7:2–3]

Incline your ear and hear the words of the
wise,
And apply your mind to my knowledge;
For it will be pleasant if you keep them
within you,
That they may be ready on your
lips. [22:17–18]

THE GRIND OF BIBLICAL ILLITERACY

Few things are more obvious and alarming in our times than biblical illiteracy. Even though the human mind is able to absorb an enormous amount of information, mental laziness remains a scandalous and undeniable fact.

So much for the bad news—the problem; let's focus, rather, on the good news—the solution. While there is not some quick-'n'-easy cure-all that will suddenly remove the grind of biblical illiteracy, I do believe that one particular discipline (more than any other) will keep us on the right road. When I began to get serious about spiritual things, it was this discipline that helped me the most. None other has come to my rescue like this one: *memorizing Scripture.*

I can still recall more than one occasion when the memorized Word of God rescued me from sexual temptation. It was as if God drew an imaginary shade (something on the order of a Venetian blind) between the other person and me, having inscribed on the surface: "Be not deceived God is not mocked; Whatever a man sows that shall he also reap" . . . a verse I committed to memory as a young teenager. During times of great loneliness, memorized Scripture has also rescued me from the pit of depression. Verses like Isaiah 41:10 and 49:15–16, along with Psalms 27:1 and 30:5 have brought me great companionship.

Before developing that concept, let's understand that we can absorb God's Word in various ways.

First, we can *hear* it. This is the simplest, least-difficult method of learning the precepts and principles of the Bible. There are plenty of trustworthy Bible teachers and preachers in our great nation. There are churches and schools, radio and TV programs, audio and video tapes, even record albums that specialize in scriptural instruction. No one in America—except those with physical hearing impairment—has any excuse for not hearing God's Word.

Second, we can *read* it. This requires more personal involvement than simply hearing the Scriptures. Those who start getting serious about their spiritual maturity buy a copy of the Bible and begin to read it. There are numerous versions, paraphrases, and styles available. Various through-the-year Bibles can be purchased, which set forth a plan that enables an individual to read through all sixty-six books of Scripture in 365 days.

Third, we can *study* it. It is at this point people begin to really mean business for God. With pen and paper, reference works, and other tools available today, the Christian starts to dig in on his (or her) own. Some take correspondence courses, others chart their own course or prefer one of the many excellent programs offered through their local church.

Fourth, we can *meditate* on it. As Scripture is heard, read, and studied, the mind becomes a reservoir of biblical truth. Those truths need to be thought through, pondered, personalized, and applied. Through times of quiet meditation, we allow the Word to seep into our cells . . . to speak to us, reprove us, warn us, comfort us. Remember those two great verses from the Book of Hebrews?

> For the word of God is living and active and sharper than any two-edged sword, and piercing as far as the division of soul and spirit, of both joints and marrow, and able to judge the thoughts and intentions of the heart. And there is no creature hidden from His sight, but all things are open and laid bare to the eyes of Him with whom we have to do. [Heb. 4:12–13]

Fifth, we can *memorize* it. What a magnificent way to replace alien and demoralizing thoughts! In all honesty, I know of no more effective way to cultivate a biblical mind and to accelerate spiritual growth than this discipline.

SOLOMON ON SCRIPTURE MEMORY

There are several sayings worth considering as we think of placing God's Word in our hearts.
Proverbs 4:4:

> Then he taught me and said to me,
> "Let your heart hold fast my words;
> Keep my commandments and live."

You'll notice the words "hold fast." In the Hebrew, the words translated "hold fast" mean "to grasp, lay hold of, seize, hold firmly." It is the verb *tah-mack,* the same term is found in Isaiah 41:10, which says:

> Do not fear, for I am with you;
> Do not anxiously look about you, for I am your God.
> I will strengthen you, surely I will help you,
> Surely I will uphold you with My righteous right hand.

The word *uphold* is from the same verb, *tah-mack.* Scripture memory gives you a grasp, a firm grip of confidence in the Bible. As God's Word gets a grip on you, it "upholds" you!
Proverbs 6:20–23:

> My son, observe the commandment of your father,
> And do not forsake the teaching of your mother;
> Bind them continually on your heart;
> Tie them around your neck.
> When you walk about, they will guide you;
> When you sleep, they will watch over you;
> And when you awake, they will talk to you.
> For the commandment is a lamp, and the teaching is light;
> And reproofs for discipline are the way of life.

Go back and locate "bind . . . tie." Scripture memory straps the truths of God to you. The word translated "bind" really means "to tie together, to bring something in league with something else." Our word *correlate* fits. Scriptures correlate so much better when we store them up. They help us come to terms with life; things make better sense when certain Scriptures are in place in our heads.

Proverbs 7:2–3:

> Keep my commandments and live,
> And my teaching as the apple of your eye.
> Bind them on your fingers;
> Write them on the tablet of your heart.

No clearer verses encouraging scripture memory could be found than these in The Proverbs. When we write something, we don't abbreviate or confuse matters. Quite the contrary, we clarify them. The Lord says "write them on the tablet of your heart." Don't be sloppy or incomplete in your memory work. It is essential that we be exact and thorough when we memorize. Without this, confidence slips away. I often think of being thorough in Scripture memory in the same way we plan a flight. Every number is precise and important (flight number, seat number, gate number) and the time as well. Being exact is extremely important!

Proverbs 22:17–18:

> Incline your ear and hear the words of the wise,
> And apply your mind to my knowledge;
> For it will be pleasant, if you keep them within you,
> That they may be ready on your lips.

I love those two sayings. They constantly encourage me to stay at this discipline! The idea of having His Word "ready on your lips" should convince us of the importance of maintaining this discipline. I say again, nothing will chase away biblical illiteracy like memorizing Scripture.

CONCLUSION

Let's conclude with three practical suggestions that have helped me in my own Scripture-memory program.

First, it is better to learn a few verses perfectly than many poorly. Learn the place (reference) as well as the words exactly as they appear in your Bible. Do not go on to another verse until you can say everything perfectly, without a glance at the Bible.

Second, review often. There is only one major secret to memory—review. In fact, it is a greater discipline to stay current in review than to take on new verses regularly.

Third, use the verse you memorize. The purpose of Scripture memory is a practical one, not academic. Who cares if you can spout off a dozen verses on temptation if you fall victim to it on a regular basis? Use your verses in prayer, in conversations and counsel with others, in correspondence, and certainly in your teaching. Use your memorized verses with your children or mate. God will bless your life *and theirs* as you tactfully share His Word. Isaiah 55:10–11 promises:

> For as the rain and the snow come down from heaven,
> And do not return there without watering the earth,
> And making it bear and sprout,
> And furnishing seed to the sower and bread to the eater;
> So shall My word be which goes forth from My mouth;
> It shall not return to Me empty,
> Without accomplishing what I desire,
> And without succeeding in the matter for which I sent it.

Caught in the grind of biblical illiteracy? Here's a good place to begin. Trust me, you will never regret the time you invest in hiding God's Word in your heart.

EFLECTIONS
ON BIBLICAL
ILLITERACY

1. Living beyond the daily grind of biblical illiteracy will not "just happen" any more than a flat tire will automatically repair itself. It will call for extra effort! To begin realistically, select six to ten verses you have come to appreciate. Perhaps you would like to use three or four from the Psalms we have looked at in Section One and several from Proverbs in this second section. Spend some time each day this week on those verses. Take them one at a time. Don't go on to the next until you have firmly committed the previous one to memory. And don't forget that the secret of Scripture memory is review.

2. As situations occur in your life where the truth of what you have memorized applies, remind yourself of it. State it aloud. Use your verse(s) also in your prayers. Share them with someone else when it is appropriate. I have found that few things bring more encouragement than the repeating of Scripture when the time is right.

3. There are Scripture-memory programs available in which you may want to enroll. One I would recommend is:

> The Navigators
> Post Office 6000
> Colorado Springs, CO 80934

Why not write today so you can get started?

Deceit is in the heart of those who devise evil, But counselors of peace have joy.   [12:20]

Anxiety in the heart of a man weighs it down, But a good word makes it glad.   [12:25]

Even in laughter the heart may be in pain, And the end of joy may be grief. The backslider in heart will have his fill of his own ways, But a good man will be satisfied with his.   [14:13–14]

Everyone who is proud in heart is an abomination to the Lord; Assuredly, he will not be unpunished.   [16:5]

The heart of the wise teaches his mouth,
And adds persuasiveness to his lips.
Pleasant words are a honeycomb,
Sweet to the soul and healing to the
    bones.   [16:23–24]

Before destruction the heart of man is
    haughty,
But humility goes before honor.   [18:12]

The foolishness of man subverts his way,
And his heart rages against the
    Lord.   [19:3]

A plan in the heart of a man is like deep
    water,
But a man of understanding draws it
    out.   [20:5]

THE GRIND OF A TROUBLED HEART

The major cause of death in our world is still heart trouble. If I were to reverse those two words, we would put our finger on a daily grind most people live with: *a troubled heart*. I realize those words are vague . . . but that's on purpose. The "troubled" heart affects us many different ways. It comes in the form of anxiety and low-grade depression. On other days it is inner churning, discontentment, feelings of insecurity, instability, often doubt, unrest, and uncertainty. A troubled heart lacks peace and often an absence of calm assurance. One answer to a troubled heart is a friend who will provide wise counsel.

The one who dubbed our era *The Aspirin Age* didn't miss it far. It's true that we live in a time when huge numbers of the world's population use aspirin or some other medication to relieve pain, much of which is stress related. But medicine cannot relieve the deep pain of a troubled heart for the multitudes who are seeking inner peace. That takes a friend who tunes in to our troubles, and precious few of us are even aware of others' struggles.

The importance of sensitivity to others' needs can scarcely be exaggerated. Even though you may not be deep in Bible knowledge, you should realize that you can be used effectively by God as a counselor, friend, and interested listener in the lives of others—just because you know the Lord Jesus Christ! Naturally, the deeper your knowledge of His Word, the sharper will be your discernment and the wiser will be your counsel. Job's counselors, for example, dealt him misery and spoke unwisely (you might take the time to read Job 13:3–4; 16:2; 21:34).

One of Solomon's sayings (Prov. 20:5) points out the value of a wise counselor.

> A plan in the heart of a man is like a deep water,
> But a man of understanding draws it out.

Look also at Proverbs 18:4:

> The words of a man's mouth are deep waters;
> The fountain of wisdom is a bubbling brook.

Those sayings tell us that there is within our inner beings a pool of water—often *troubled* water! Also notice that the mouth brings forth the substance of that pool thanks to the *man of understanding* who draws it out.

For example, you may feel deeply about the circumstances in which you find yourself. You cannot fully think through the depths of your feelings without the aid of one who "draws out" those feelings. And how important it is to have such people nearby!

Does that describe *you*? If so, you will be willing to take the time that is necessary to minister in this way. Personally, I believe this is exactly what Paul has in mind when he writes: "Bear one another's burdens, and thus fulfill the law of Christ" (Gal. 6:2).

Because the daily grind of a troubled heart is so common, we tend to overlook it in others. We often think we're the only ones who struggle with it. Not so! It's all around us. And as I mentioned earlier, it wears many faces. For example, I find these six specified in Solomon's sayings:

1. A "deceitful" heart.

> Deceit is in the heart of those who devise evil,
> But counselors of peace have joy. [12:20]

2. A "heavy" heart.

> Anxiety in the heart of a man weighs it down,
> But a good word makes it glad. [12:25]

The Hebrew verb from which *anxiety* is translated, literally means "to be anxious, fearful, worried." You can detect a worried heart rather easily. It shows up on one's face.

3. A "sorrowful" heart.

> Even in laughter the heart may be in pain,
> And the end of joy may be grief. [14:13]

4. A "backsliding" heart (carnality).

The backslider in heart will have his fill of his own ways,
But a good man will be satisfied with his. [14:14]

5. A "proud" heart.

Everyone who is proud in heart is an abomination to the Lord;
Assuredly, he will not be unpunished. [16:5]

Before destruction the heart of man is haughty,
But humility goes before honor. [18:12]

6. An "angry" heart.

> The foolishness of man subverts his way,
> And his heart rages against the Lord. [19:3]

Perhaps you wonder *how* you can detect these troubles. Look at Proverbs 20:11–12:

> It is by his deeds that a lad distinguishes himself
> If his conduct is pure and right.
> The hearing ear and the seeing eye,
> The Lord has made both of them.

As you notice, the Lord says He has given you hearing ears and seeing eyes. I urge you to *use them!* Listen carefully. Watch the person with whom you speak. Be sensitive. This, of course, implies that *you* talk very little, especially during the initial contact. Now read Proverbs 16:23–24:

> The heart of the wise teaches his mouth,
> And adds persuasiveness to his lips.
> Pleasant words are a honeycomb,
> Sweet to the soul and healing to the bones.

God will be pleased to use your words as His instruments, if you allow Him to control what you say. It would be wise of you to claim the promise God gave to Moses in Exodus 4:12: "Now then go, and I, even I, will be with your mouth, and teach you what you are to say." Claim that all week long.

Who knows? You may be the one God wants to use this week in the life of another who can't seem to get beyond the grind of a troubled heart.

EFLECTIONS ON
A TROUBLED HEART

1. This week is a good time to stop, look, and listen.

   a. *Stop* long enough to pray. Ask God for His wisdom to see beyond the grind . . . to realize you are not alone in your troubles . . . to have a renewed sense of inner relief.
   b. *Look* around. Become aware of the circle of acquaintances that is larger than your own personal world. Be sensitive. Discern turmoil in others . . . even in your friends.
   c. *Listen.* Instead of launching a barrage of verbal missiles, just ask a few questions, then (without offering advice) listen. Patiently and graciously hear them out. When our words are few, they become more valuable.

2. Go back to those six examples of a troubled heart from Proverbs. Which one is *your* most frequent battle? Does anybody know it? Can you say you are truly accountable? Have you given anyone permission to step into your private world? Just as others need a "counselor-friend," so do you. How about reaching out and asking someone you respect and trust to enter your secret world? Yes, you'll need to choose the person(s) carefully . . . but begin the search this week.

3. Check out a reliable book on counseling from a local library or preferably your church library. Begin reading it soon. Think of ways to implement some of the techniques presented in the book. One word of caution, however: Be sure that the author is committed to biblical principles and truly loves Christ as Lord. It is so important that we know a counselor's underlying faith before we embrace the concepts and techniques he (or she) espouses.

There are six things which the
Lord hates,
Yes, seven which are an
abomination to Him:
Haughty eyes, a lying tongue,
And hands that shed innocent blood,
A heart that devises wicked plans,
Feet that run rapidly to evil,
A false witness who utters lies,
And one who spreads strife among
brothers.   [6:16–19]

The tongue of the wise makes knowledge
acceptable,
But the mouth of fools spouts
folly.   [15:2]

The lips of the wise spread knowledge,
But the hearts of fools are not so.   [15:7]

THE GRIND OF AN UNCONTROLLED TONGUE

(PART ONE)

Solomon's sayings have a lot to say about what we say. In fact, "tongue," "mouth," "lips," and "words" are mentioned in Proverbs almost 150 times. That means on an average of just under five times in each of the thirty-one chapters, those words occur. Seems to me any subject mentioned that often calls for at least two weeks of our attention. Let's do that.

A key statement on the subject of the tongue is located in Proverbs 15:2, which says:

> The tongue of the wise makes knowledge acceptable,
> But the mouth of fools spouts folly.

That's one of those "contrastive couplets," isn't it? It mentions "the wise" in contrast to "fools." Interestingly, the way they use their tongues is a dead giveaway of their identity. You and I realize, of course, that the root problem is not in the mouth but in the heart—the person deep within us. Jesus taught that:

> "The good man out of the good treasure of his heart brings forth what is good; and the evil man out of the evil treasure brings forth what is evil; for his mouth speaks from that which fills his heart." [Luke 6:45]

Like a bucket draws water from a well, so the tongue dips down and pours out whatever is in the heart. If the source is clean, that is what the tongue communicates. If it is contaminated, again, the tongue will expose it.

Using the key statement of Proverbs 15:2 as our outline, let's focus this week on the wrong uses of our tongue . . . and next week on the right uses.

I have never known anyone who has not at some time struggled with using his (or her) tongue in a wrong manner *or* who has not suffered the brunt of another's tongue. Few grinds are more painful!

As I read through Solomon's sayings, I find at least five unhealthy ways an uncontrolled tongue reveals itself. If this issue of an uncontrolled tongue is one of your "daily grinds," let me urge you to pay close attention.

1. Deceitful flattery.

> Bread obtained by falsehood is sweet to a man,
> But afterward his mouth will be filled with gravel. [20:17]

> He who rebukes a man will afterward find more favor
> Than he who flatters with the tongue. [28:23]

What is flattery? Nothing more than insincere compliments expressed with deceitful motives. It is excessive praise verbalized in hopes of gaining favor in the eyes of another. A good rule to follow: Don't do it. Stay clear of it. In fact, it is better to rebuke another in love than to flatter deceitfully.

2. Gossip and slander.

> A worthless person, a wicked man,
> Is the one who walks with a false mouth,
> Who winks with his eyes, who signals with his feet,
> Who points with his fingers;
> Who with perversity in his heart devises evil continually,
> Who spreads strife. [6:12–14]

> He who conceals hatred has lying lips,
> And he who spreads slander is a fool. [10:18]

> A fool's mouth is his ruin,
> And his lips are the snare of his soul.
> The words of a whisperer are like dainty morsels,
> And they go down into the innermost parts of the body. [18:7–8]

He who goes about as a slanderer reveals secrets,
Therefore do not associate with a gossip. [20:19]

Who hasn't been hurt by the uncontrolled tongue of a gossip? But wait. What, exactly, is meant by gossip? It is a false or exaggerated report maliciously discussed and/or circulated about a person. Throughout Scripture, God reserves some of His severest words for gossips as He condemns this habit.

I would also include here the importance of confidentiality. Those who can be trusted with sensitive information are rare!

3. Arguments, striving, angry words. Take the time to read Proverbs 14:16–17; 15:4; 17:14; 18:6; 25:15; 29:11. You'd also profit from a careful examination of the following sayings:

Do not associate with a man given to anger;
Or go with a hot-tempered man,
Lest you learn his ways,
And find a snare for yourself. [22:24–25]

An angry man stirs up strife,
And a hot-tempered man abounds in transgression. [29:22]

By "arguments" and "striving" I do *not* mean the expression of differing opinions or even disagreement. Intelligent thinking and unguarded, open conversation include the freedom of expression, which involves periodic differences of opinion. Arguments and striving, however, have to do with attitudes such as stubbornness and rigidity. This inevitably arouses anger—the kind of anger that is displeasing to the Lord. It is not so much a question of *do* you disagree, but *how* you disagree.

How easy to form the habit of striving! Haven't you seen husbands and wives who argue, simply out of habit? Entire homes are set on edge when this attitude pervades.

Read over each proverb listed above. If they describe you, your homework is overdue!

4. Boasting and foolish jesting. First, let's consider *boasting*. The next two verses will help clarify what I mean:

> In the mouth of the foolish is a rod for his back,
> But the lips of the wise will preserve them. [14:3]

> Like clouds and wind without rain
> Is a man who boasts of his gifts falsely. [25:14]

It is subtle how we shine our own halos. How desperately we want to be noticed! We hint about it, we "feed" on compliments, we even brag with spiritual phrases, yet we know that our hidden motive is to exalt ourselves.

Link all this with Proverbs 6:16–17:

> There are six things which the Lord hates,
> Yes, seven which are an abomination to Him:
> Haughty eyes, a lying tongue. . . .

Listed first on God's "hate list" are haughty eyes. And haughty eyes are the indication of a prideful spirit so often seen in those who boast.

Now, let's address *foolish jesting*. Read Proverbs 10:21; 15:7; 18:7. Ponder especially 18:7:

> A fool's mouth is his ruin,
> And his lips are the snare of his soul.

By "foolish talk" I have in mind talk that is not edifying— silly, useless, foul and/or profane verbiage. (I'm certainly not including tasteful and wholesome humor.) God warns us that the lips of the fool are the "snare" of his soul. How often we have been snared!

A verse from the Letter to the Ephesians vividly warns us:

> Let no unwholesome word proceed from your mouth, but only such a word as is good for edification according to the need of the moment, that it may give grace to those who hear. [4:29]

5. Verbosity.

> When there are many words, transgression is unavoidable,
> But he who restrains his lips is wise. [10:19]

Verbosity means excess verbiage—talking too much and saying too little. One who is verbose usually feels compelled to give his comment. He is also "hard of listening." He feels constrained to fill silent segments of conversation with talk, words without significance. He interrupts without hesitation. A number of years ago I discovered that I never learned anything while I was talking. Neither do you!

We have been thinking about the wrong uses of our tongue. The scene has not been pleasant; has it? I hope that rehearsing these five unpleasant examples will encourage you to put the clamps on the muscle in your mouth. Next week, let's focus on some correct, healthy uses of the tongue. Frankly, I'm ready for the positive. Aren't you?

EFLECTIONS ON AN UNCONTROLLED TONGUE

(PART ONE)

This has been enormously convicting! Since that is true, let's consider three *brief* reflections for the week.

1. Think before you say anything. If it won't contribute, say nothing.

2. Each morning this week, as you look at yourself in the bathroom mirror, don't forget to look at your *tongue*. Hold your mouth open long enough to realize that slab of skin, membranes, and muscles has the power to injure . . . to stab . . . to kill. Pray for control.

3. Cultivate the lost art of listening all week long. Deliberately talk less. By the end of the week you'll be amazed at how much you have learned!

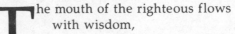

T he mouth of the righteous flows
with wisdom,
But the perverted tongue will be
cut out.
The lips of the righteous bring forth what
is acceptable,
But the mouth of the wicked, what is
perverted.   [10:31–32]

The eyes of the Lord are in every place,
Watching the evil and the good.   [15:3]

A man has joy in an apt answer,
And how delightful is a timely
word!   [15:23]

Bright eyes gladden the heart;
Good news puts fat on the bones.
He whose ear listens to the life-giving
reproof
Will dwell among the wise.   [15:30–31]

Pleasant words are a honeycomb,
Sweet to the soul and healing to the
    bones.   [16:24]

A joyful heart is good medicine,
But a broken spirit dries up the bones.
    [17:22]

Like apples of gold in settings of silver
Is a word spoken in right circumstances.
Like an earring of gold and an ornament
    of fine gold
Is a wise reprover to a listening
    ear.   [25:11–12]

Better is open rebuke
Than love that is concealed.
Faithful are the wounds of a friend,
But deceitful are the kisses of an
    enemy.   [27:5–6]

THE GRIND OF AN UNCONTROLLED TONGUE

(PART TWO)

Since Solomon says so much about the tongue, it was impossible to digest all that wisdom during one week's time. And since this slippery little fellow we call the tongue gives us so much trouble so often, it seemed appropriate to return to the subject for a second look. After all, James 3:2 states:

> For we all stumble in many ways. If anyone does not stumble in what he says, he is a perfect man, able to bridle the whole body as well.

In other words, a controlled tongue is the hallmark of maturity. And how few there are, it seems, who qualify!

All last week we gave thought to some of the unwholesome and detrimental uses of the tongue. We uncovered no fewer than five wrong ways the tongue can be used:

1. Deceitful flattery
2. Gossip and slander
3. Arguments, strife, and angry words
4. Boasting and foolish jesting
5. Verbosity

What a convicting list! As a matter of fact, I know of very few subjects *more* convicting than this one.

But there certainly are right ways the tongue can be used. This week, let's focus on those as we let Solomon's sayings add soothing oil to the daily grind of an uncontrolled tongue. You may recall Solomon's saying from Proverbs 15:2, 7, which we looked at last week:

> The tongue of the wise makes knowledge acceptable,
> But the mouth of fools spouts folly.
>
> The lips of the wise spread knowledge.

Just as we found five wrong uses, there are also five ways "the lips of the wise" can bring benefit to others.

1. <u>Wise counsel and sound advice.</u>

> The lips of the righteous bring forth what is acceptable. [10:32]
>
> The lips of the wise spread knowledge. . . . [15:7]
>
> Without consultation, plans are frustrated,
> But with many counselors they succeed. [15:22]
>
> Prepare plans by consultation,
> And make war by wise guidance. [20:18]

It would also be worth your time to read and meditate on Proverbs 25:19, 26, and 28. These three additional sayings look at the results of listening to unwise, unsound advice. We have all experienced both sides of counsel—wise and unwise. How can anyone adequately measure the great benefits of wise, timely counsel?

Obviously, one without God cannot give you God's viewpoint, even though he may have beneficial words of human wisdom. We must use great discernment when seeking others' counsel. You may be surprised to read that not even the aged are always reliable:

> The abundant in years may not be wise,
> Nor may elders understand justice. [Job 32:9]

2. <u>Reproof, rebuke, spiritual exhortation.</u>

> A fool rejects his father's discipline,
> But he who regards reproof is prudent. [Prov. 15:5]

Stern discipline is for him who forsakes the way;
He who hates reproof will die. [15:10]

He whose ear listens to the life-giving reproof
Will dwell among the wise.
He who neglects discipline despises himself,
But he who listens to reproof acquires understanding. [15:31–32]

Faithful are the wounds of a friend,
But deceitful are the kisses of an enemy. [27:6]

He who rebukes a man will afterward find more favor
Than he who flatters with the tongue. [28:23]

How rare yet how essential reproof is! Can't you think of occasions when someone wisely yet firmly rebuked you . . . and you became a better person because of it? Look again at Proverbs 27:6. I will amplify it, using the Hebrew text as a basis for my words:

Trustworthy are the bruises caused by the wounding of one who loves you; deceitful is the flattery of one who hates you.

This tells us several things:

- The one who does the rebuking should be one who *loves* the one he rebukes.

- The "bruise" that is left lingers on. It is not soon forgotten.

- Friendship should include the freedom to mention a criticism.

- Not all compliments come from the right motive.

So much of this matter has to do with discernment and discretion. There is the right *way* and the right *time* (not to mention the right *motive*) for such an act. God certainly is not pleased with criticism and/or rebuke from anyone and everyone at any time he pleases.

No finer passage of Scripture on the subject of timing our words can be found than Proverbs 25:11–12:

Like apples of gold in settings of silver
Is a word spoken in right circumstances.
Like an earring of gold and an ornament of fine gold
Is a wise reprover to a listening ear.

3. Words of encouragement.

A man has joy in an apt answer,
And how delightful is a timely word! [15:23]

Bright eyes gladden the heart;
Good news puts fat on the bones. [15:30]

Pleasant words are a honeycomb,
Sweet to the soul and healing to the bones. [16:24]

By "encouragement" I mean sincere expressions of gratitude given honestly to another individual (usually in private). We so seldom do this, yet it is one of the signs of a mature, godly individual.

Do you express encouragement to those closest to you? Your wife or husband? How about your children? Your teacher? Your secretary? Someone who does a quality job for you? However, we should guard against doing it *too much.* That cheapens the encouragement and makes it appear insincere. Like too large a gem on a ring, encouragement, when overdone, lacks elegance and charm.

4. Witnessing, teaching, comforting.

The mouth of the righteous is a fountain of life. . . . [10:11]

The tongue of the righteous is as choice silver,
The heart of the wicked is worth little.
The lips of the righteous feed many,
But fools die for lack of understanding. [10:20–21]

The fruit of the righteous is a tree of life,
And he who is wise wins souls. [11:30]

The words of a man's mouth are deep waters;
The fountain of wisdom is a bubbling brook. [18:4]

Death and life are in the power of the tongue [18:21a]

Deliver those who are being taken away to death,
And those who are staggering to slaughter, O hold them back.
If you say, "See, we did not know this,"
Does He not consider it who weighs the hearts?
And does He not know it who keeps your soul?
And will He not render to man according to his work? [24:11–12]

Who can accurately measure the benefits gleaned from the tongue of a godly teacher, well-versed in the Scriptures? Or, how could we gauge the depth of comfort received from the lips of a close friend during a period of grief or affliction? And what about the one(s) who told you about Christ? Remember the help you received from the gloriously good news of the Lord Jesus Christ? My, what a tremendous help!

Stop and consider this: The gospel is believed *only* when words have communicated it. The words may be written or spoken, but words are an integral part of the plan. To one who shares Christ, the tongue is essential.

Your tongue can serve no better function in life than that of faithfully, consistently communicating Christ.

5. A good sense of humor.

> A joyful heart makes a cheerful face,
> But when the heart is sad, the spirit is broken. [15:13]

> All the days of the afflicted are bad,
> But a cheerful heart has a continual feast. [15:15]

By a sense of humor, please understand that I am *not* referring to silly, foolish talk or to distasteful, and ill-timed jesting. By humor, I mean well-chosen, properly timed expressions of wit and amusing, funny statements. I am so convinced of the value of wholesome humor, I believe one who lacks it will not be as capable a leader or as good a communicator as he (or she) could be.

There are special times when a sense of humor is needed, such as in lengthy, tense, and heated meetings, or when a serious atmosphere has settled in the home over a long period of time, or following extremely difficult experiences in our lives.

How quickly and how easily we forget to laugh! And yet, how healthy laughter is. Look at that last phrase of the final saying I quoted above. The Hebrew text literally says that the cheerful heart *"causes good healing."*

How do you measure up, my friend? Honestly now, have you become so serious you can no longer enjoy yourself (and others)? Let's face it, if there is one, general criticism we Christians must accept without argument, it is that we have become altogether too serious about everything in life. We exclude or ignore most every opportunity for a good, healthy laugh! We're "uptight," far too intense, and much too critical of ourselves and others. As a result, our tolerance and understanding are extremely limited. May God loosen us up! And may He ultimately enable us to live beyond the grind of an uncontrolled tongue.

EFLECTIONS ON AN UNCONTROLLED TONGUE

(PART TWO)

1. Turn to the New Testament in your Bible and read James 3:1–12 slowly and aloud. Do that *at least three times* this week. After each reading, sit quietly and talk with the Lord about how much you want Him to gain full control over your tongue.

2. Make a list of two ways you could use your tongue in a more helpful manner.

   (a) _____

   _____

   (b) _____

   _____

   How about implementing both before the week is over?

3. A final suggestion *must* deal with improving your sense of humor. In all honesty, have you become rather testy? Maybe a bit too tedious, even negative? Perhaps it is due to too many hours at work. Burnout always robs us of our humor. It may stem from your serious temperament or your circumstances. Enough of that! Take a few extra hours off this weekend. Deliberately focus on the brighter side of life. Select a humorous book to read or a comedy on television or at the movies . . . and let your hair down! People who cultivate a healthy sense of humor give themselves permission to enjoy life. Start there.

Better is a dish of vegetables where
    love is,
Than a fattened ox and hatred
    with it.   [15:17]

———————————

Better is a little with righteousness
Than great income with injustice.   [16:8]

———————————

Better is a dry morsel and quietness with
    it
Than a house full of feasting with
    strife.   [17:1]

THE GRIND OF
DISCONTENTMENT

Many folks eat their hearts out, suffering from the contagious "If Only" disease. Its germs infect every slice of life.

> If only I had more money
> If only I could make better grades
> If only we owned a nicer home
> If only we hadn't made that bad investment
> If only I hadn't come from such a bad background
> If only she would have stayed married to me
> If only our pastor were a stronger preacher
> If only my child were able to walk
> If only we could have children
> If only we *didn't* have children
> If only the business could have succeeded
> If only my husband hadn't died so young
> If only I would've said "No" to drugs
> If only they had given me a break
> If only I hadn't had that accident
> If only we could get back on our feet
> If only he would ask me out
> If only people would accept me as I am
> If only my folks hadn't divorced
> If only I had more friends

The list is endless. Woven through the fabric of all those words is a sigh that comes from the daily grind of discontentment. Taken far enough, it leads to the dead-end street of self-pity—

one of the most distasteful and inexcusable of all attitudes. Discontentment is one of those daily grinds that forces others to listen to our list of woes. But they don't for long! Discontented souls soon become lonely souls.

I am so pleased that Solomon did not overlook discontentment. On three separate occasions he wrote sayings for all of us to read, especially when we are tempted to feel sorry for ourselves. You may have already noticed that all three are "comparative couplets" where the former things named are "better than" the latter. For example:

> Better is a dish of vegetables where love is,
> Than a fattened ox and hatred with it. [15:17]

Who needs a T-bone steak? So what's the big deal about chateaubriand for two if it must be eaten in an absence of love? Several years ago I smiled as I read about a gal at a cocktail party trying to look happy. A friend noticed the huge sparkling rock on her finger and gushed, "My! What a gorgeous diamond!"

"Yes," she admitted, "it's a Callahan diamond. It comes with the Callahan curse."

"The Callahan curse?" asked her friend. "What's that?"

"Mr. Callahan," she said with a frown.

Solomon asks, "What good is it to have more and more of anything if hatred is part of the package?"

Here's another eloquent rebuke:

> Better is a dry morsel and quietness with it
> Than a house full of feasting with strife. [17:1]

We've seen that, too. Lots of people and partying, constant coming and going, endless activity and loads of food . . . but strife. No thanks. How easy to be fooled by all the noise and smoke! A simple bowl of oatmeal served in a tranquil setting is far better.

> Better is a little with righteousness
> Than great income with injustice. [16:8]

Can't miss the point of that one either. Anything—*anything*—that requires injustice to get won't bring satisfaction. Just "a little" with righteousness outstrips the Taj Mahal with injustice. Who cares if his bank account is stuffed and his investment portfolio is impressive if he has to live with a guilty conscience? It's like sleeping on a coat hanger. Every move you make is another reminder that something is wrong.

The rich *and* the poor must hear this. Those who want (and have) much and those who feel they need more are equally in need of this counsel. Discontentment rarely has anything to do with one's financial status. Greed is cancer of the attitude, not caused by insufficient funds but by inappropriate objectives. Some will *never* be satisfied, no matter how much they have. Discontentment is a sneaky thief who continues to disrupt our peace and to steal our happiness. Ever so subtly it whispers "more . . . more . . . more . . . more . . ."

Look at the words of 1 Timothy 6:6–10, 17–19 very carefully, as if you are reading them for the first time:

> But godliness actually is a means of great gain, when accompanied by contentment. For we have brought nothing into the world, so we cannot take anything out of it either. And if we have food and covering, with these we shall be content. But those who want to get rich fall into temptation and a snare and many foolish and harmful desires which plunge men into ruin and destruction. For the love of money is a root of all sorts of evil, and some by longing for it have wandered away from the faith, and pierced themselves with many a pang. . . .

> Instruct those who are rich in this present world not to be conceited or to fix their hope on the uncertainty of riches, but on God, who richly supplies us with all things to enjoy. Instruct them to do good, to be rich in good works, to be generous and ready to share, storing up for themselves the treasure of a good foundation for the future, so that they may take hold of that which is life indeed.

As the Chinese philosopher Lao-Tzu once said:

> There is no calamity greater than lavish desires.
> There is no greater guilt than discontentment.
> And there is no greater disaster than greed.

 EFLECTIONS ON
DISCONTENTMENT

1. As you read through that "if only" list, perhaps *your* particular discontentment was missing. If so, acknowledge it here. Openly admit the one longing you have nursed for most of your life.

2. Now go back and read those words from the Chinese philosopher. How do they apply? In what way can you say you are willing to address your secret longing? And while we're at it, is there ever a proper place for being discontented? Explain your answer, especially in light of the words "if we have food and covering . . . be content."

3. Jesus, on more than a few occasions, spoke directly to the issue of always wanting more. In His immortal Sermon on the Mount, He stated "You cannot serve God and mammon" (Matt. 6:24). What is the difference between "earning" and "serving" money? One more thought: If Jesus were to live on earth today, where do you think He would be employed? What kind of car would He drive? How much money would He earn? Do you think He would periodically fly first class? Would He ever feel a slight sting of discontentment? Why? Or why not?

For the commandment is a lamp,
    and the teaching is light;
    And reproofs for discipline are the
    way of life,
To keep you from the evil woman,
From the smooth tongue of the
    adulteress.
Do not desire her beauty in your heart,
Nor let her catch you with her eyelids.
For on account of a harlot one is reduced
    to a loaf of bread,
And an adulteress hunts for the precious
    life.
Can a man take fire in his bosom,
And his clothes not be burned?
Or can a man walk on hot coals,
And his feet not be scorched?
So is the one who goes in to his
    neighbor's wife;
Whoever touches her will not go
    unpunished.   [6:23–29]

The one who commits adultery with a
    woman is lacking sense;
He who would destroy himself does it.
Wounds and disgrace he will find,
And his reproach will not be blotted
    out.   [6:32–33]

THE GRIND OF LUSTFUL TEMPTATIONS

Solomon shoots straight.

I find that rather refreshing in our day of gray definitions and bold rationalizations. The sayings you just read are timeless and no less relevant today than they were when the ink was still wet. Our battle with lustful temptations is intense. There is always the opportunity to fall . . . the snares to trip us up. Whether it's in the area of fortune, fame, power, or pleasure— lust wages a mighty war in our souls. And many there are who surrender to it.

Let me remind you that these words and warnings appear in another of the "My son" accounts. As a father, Solomon wanted to leave trustworthy counsel for his son to read and heed. Perhaps he wrote these words with an extra amount of passion since his own father David had suffered the consequence of yielding to lustful temptations many years earlier. Though David's adultery happened before Solomon's birth, no one can doubt that he was ever aware of the consequences that came in the wake of the king's compromise. Solomon was reared in a context that never let him forget his father's moral failure.

Solomon begins with the standard of Holy Scripture:

> For the commandment is a lamp, and the teaching is light;
> And reproofs for discipline are the way of life. [6:23]

That is always the place to find one's standard . . . God's perfect and Holy Word. Not the media. Not others' opinions.

Not the books written by fellow strugglers. Not even our own conscience, which can be seared, calloused, or prejudiced. The "lamp" of God's precepts, the "light" of His teaching—*these* provide us with unfailing direction. Furthermore, as we learned earlier, His reproofs goad us into line and intensify our discipline.

So then, what do we learn from Solomon's sayings when we're faced with the lure of a lustful lifestyle? How do we live beyond the grind of this kind of temptation?

1. Stay away from "the evil woman" (or man).

2. Guard against the "smooth tongue" that invites you in.

3. Refuse to entertain secret desires of the opposite sex's beauty.

4. Don't let those alluring eyes captivate you.

Now, wait just a minute! *Why* would Solomon take such a hard stand on resisting lust's appeal? Without the slightest hesitation, the wise man sets forth the truth, which so few stop to think through today. As we read these sayings, we find several specific reasons:

First, the adulteress goes for "the precious life," which, when snared, is reduced to zero. The backwash is undeniable. To name only a few of the consequences:

Loss of character	Injury to his career
Loss of self-respect	Smearing of his name
Loss of others' respect	Embarrassment to his church
Loss of his family	Draining of his finances
Loss of his testimony	Possibility of disease
Loss of his joy and peace	Beginning of secrecy

Second, the hot fire of punishment will begin and never be fully extinguished. Burn scars are among the most obvious and painful. The one who yields to lustful temptations "will not go unpunished."

Third, it reveals the "lack of sense"; a self-destructive process is begun.

Fourth, "wounds and disgrace" will never be fully erased. Solomon isn't through!

He goes even further, describing in lurid detail how lust appears so appealing, so accepting, so safe . . . yet in the end, it is like "an arrow" and "a snare."

At the window of my house I looked out through the lattice. I saw among the simple, I noticed among the young men, a youth who lacked judgment. He was going down the street near her corner, walking along in the direction of her house at twilight, as the day was fading, as the dark of night set in.

Then out came a woman to meet him, dressed like a prostitute and with crafty intent. (She is loud and defiant, her feet never stay at home; now in the street, now in the squares, at every corner she lurks.) She took hold of him and kissed him and with a brazen face she said: "I have peace offerings at home; today I fulfilled my vows. So I came out to meet you; I looked for you and have found you! I have covered my bed with colored linens from Egypt. I have perfumed my bed with myrrh, aloes and cinnamon. Come, let's drink deep of love till morning; let's enjoy ourselves with love! My husband is not at home; he has gone on a long journey. He took his purse filled with money and will not be home till full moon."

With persuasive words she led him astray; she seduced him with her smooth talk. All at once he followed her like an ox going to the slaughter, like a deer stepping into a noose till an arrow pierces his liver, like a bird darting into a snare, little knowing it will cost him his life. [Prov. 7:6–23, NIV]

Wake up! Let the truth be heard, my friend. When the escapade ends, gross consequences follow . . . and *they* never end.

This is a day when many are becoming soft on those who fall morally. At the risk of overkill, let me ask you: Do you find Solomon soft? Stop and meditate on the final six words in the scripture you just read: ". . . it will cost him his life." I call that about as severe a consequence as one can imagine.

Now is the time to come to terms with temptation. The daily grind may not fully go away, but it need not be considered an overwhelming battle.

REFLECTIONS ON LUSTFUL TEMPTATIONS

1. Because Solomon shoots straight, I see no reason to back off and trade diplomacy for truth. A good place to start is with a few pointed questions:

   - Are you flirting with lust or resisting it? Do you encourage sexual come-ons?

   - Have you worked out a plan for lust to keep a foot in the door? Be painfully honest.

   - Is there some secret sin you are harboring? Someone you're meeting with? Magazines? Video cassettes? How about those hotel late-night TV movies? Or cable television channels?

   I plead with you; run for your life from those flames of temptation. If you don't, they are sure to grow hotter as the months pass.

2. You may be dangerously close to sexual fire. It could be so close that you find yourself unable to back off. It may call for professional help. *Get it.* Contact a pastor for reference if you don't know whom to see . . . or call someone you respect and start back toward purity. Let me urge you, also, to burn whatever you have hidden away—make a *clean* sweep of it! Tell your illicit partner it is over. Do that even if you don't feel like doing it. Act now.

3. I have already mentioned the importance of being accountable. Once again, I must affirm how valuable it would be
   for you to allow another trusted individual (or two) into
   the secret chambers of your life. In order for this to happen, you need to be the one who makes the first move.
   Even if you don't have a major battle in this area, you *still
   need a point of accountability.* An accountability group
   forms a safety net. A few trusted friends who love you too
   much to let you exist in a self-made world of secret struggles and personal blind spots can become your best in-
   surance investment. Living beyond the daily grind of
   lustful temptations will require team effort. Start building
   your team!

Go to the ant, O sluggard,
Observe her ways and be wise,
Which, having no chief,
Officer or ruler,
Prepares her food in the summer,
And gathers her provision in the harvest.
How long will you lie down, O sluggard?
When will you arise from your sleep?
"A little sleep, a little slumber,
A little folding of the hands to rest"—
And your poverty will come in like a
    vagabond,
And your need like an armed
    man. [6:6–11]

The soul of the sluggard craves and gets
    nothing,
But the soul of the diligent is made
    fat. [13:4]

Commit your works to the Lord,
And your plans will be
    established. [16:3]

The mind of man plans his way,
But the Lord directs his steps. [16:9]

Do not love sleep, lest you become poor;
Open your eyes, and you will be satisfied
    with food. [20:13]

The plans of the diligent lead surely to
    advantage,
But everyone who is hasty comes surely
    to poverty. [21:5]

THE GRIND OF PROCRASTINATION

Pro·cras·ti·nate: To put off intentionally and habitually, postpone . . . to put off . . . reprehensibly the doing of something that should be done.

—Webster's Seventh New Collegiate Dictionary

Thanks, Webster.

Not that we needed a definition, but sometimes it helps to nail things down. When we procrastinate, we deliberately say "later" but usually think "never." It's the mañana syndrome: "Someday, we gotta get organized." Which, being interpreted, is really saying, "Who cares if it *ever* gets done?" People who procrastinate have no definite plans to accomplish the objective. They simply push it into the slimy ooze of indefiniteness, that murky swamp where the thought of good intentions slips in over its head.

Is your daily grind procrastination? Then Solomon's sayings to the rescue!

First off, Solomon assures us that we have all the mental equipment we need to do the deed.

> The plans of the heart belong to man,
> But the answer of the tongue is from the Lord. [16:1]

That ability to plan is unique to mankind. "Orderly thinking" (16:1, MLB) is ours and ours alone. We have a built-in capacity to think things through . . . to plan things out. Horses don't. Rabbits can't. Chickens won't. But you and I can *and should.*

Second, Solomon affirms we can also have the *desire* to get the thing done.

> Commit your works to the Lord,
> And your plans will be established. [16:3]

We even have divine assistance available. But please don't kid yourself; this is not automatic. A desire doesn't guarantee accomplishment. I recall another saying of Solomon:

> The soul of the sluggard craves and gets nothing,
> But the soul of the diligent is made fat. [13:4]

Deep within our beings rest rival foes: Sluggard vs. Diligence. The fight is on. Both have desires, you understand. Even Sluggard "craves," but he accomplishes zilch. He doesn't follow through. He postpones: "Maybe someday."
But Diligence?

> The plans of the diligent lead surely to advantage,
> But everyone who is hasty comes surely to poverty. [21:5]

Then why don't we always overrule Sluggard and give the nod to Diligence? Why do we opt for procrastination more often than not? I have thought about that a lot (even while sitting here, realizing I needed to get at it). Here are my conclusions:

- Either we set goals that were unwise or unrealistic
- Or we attempted to do something that was not God's will
- Or we allowed Sluggard to win when he arm-wrestled Diligence!

So? Surprisingly, Solomon says we need to take a trip out to an anthill. In fact, God *commands* us to do so!

> Go to the ant, O sluggard,
> Observe her ways and be wise,

> Which, having no chief, officer or ruler,
> Prepares her food in the summer,
> And gathers her provision in the harvest.
> How long will you lie down, O sluggard?
> When will you arise from your sleep? [6:6–10]

Ouch! I find it more than a little humiliating to think of standing six feet above a tiny insect and being told to bend down and learn from its ways. But what lessons the ant teaches us! Those tiny pedagogues model several valuable messages:

- They don't need some superintendent over them.
- They get the essentials done first.
- They work ahead of time so they can relax later.
- They do it all without fanfare or applause.

What happens if we fail to follow the ant's example?

- We continue to procrastinate.
- We begin to resemble "a vagabond."
- We ultimately become dependent on others.

Furthermore, we miss one of life's most delightful rewards, which Solomon describes in these words:

> Hope deferred makes the heart sick,
> But desire fulfilled is a tree of life. . . .
> Desire realized is sweet to the soul. [Prov. 13:12, 19]

Our hearts get "sick" when we keep putting our hope on hold. What is it that is so "sweet to the soul"? Accomplishment. For example:

- A garage cleaned spic and span.
- The storm windows attached before winter's first blast.
- Those twenty pounds gone from our bodies.
- The whole yard mowed . . . and trimmed.
- The room addition finished (yes, that includes *paint!*).
- A car waxed.
- A new dress made.
- Pictures labeled and placed in the photo album.
- The chapter written!

EFLECTIONS ON PROCRASTINATION

1. Take the Scriptures literally. Go out to the closest anthill and watch. Watch very carefully. If you look closely you will see those tiny creatures handling a load much larger and heavier than their own bodies. Furthermore, you'll see none of them kicking back, arguing with each other, or procrastinating. Diligent creatures, those ants.

2. Perhaps what keeps most of us from getting a big job done is one of two things:

    a. Getting started
    b. Spelling out a plan

    Think about both for a few moments. Why not plunge in right away? Better still, how about writing down a procedure. Organize the workload—you know the age-old motto: Plan your work, then work your plan. That's not very clever or creative, but it is still effective.

3. Fill in the blanks:

    • I need to finish _____.
    • What keeps me from it is _____
    _____
    and _____.
    • By _____ (time) on _____ (date), I will complete that project.

    When you do, reward yourself! Your "realized desire" deserves loud applause.

B y wisdom a house is built,
And by understanding it is
   established;
And by knowledge the rooms are
   filled
With all precious and pleasant
   riches.   [24:3–4]

THE GRIND OF DOMESTIC DISHARMONY

Of all the "grinds" that eat away at our peace, none is more nagging, more draining, more painful than disharmony at home. The sarcastic infighting. The negative putdowns. The stinging stares. The volatile explosions of anger . . . occasionally, even brutality and abuse. A TV blaring in the living room, a stack of dishes in the sink. Doors slammed shut. Desperate feelings of loneliness.

Those descriptions may portray the dwelling where you live. It is possible that you have gotten to the place where you look for excuses not to be there, or to be home only as little as possible. You sometimes wonder what can be done to restore harmony . . . to make things different. You probably think that change is impossible. I have good news: It is not.

Solomon, in two simple-sounding verses (24:3–4), tells us we need three essential ingredients in order to turn a house into a home—but what powerful ingredients they are!

1. "By *wisdom* a house is built. . . ."

Wisdom is seeing with discernment. The original Hebrew word emphasizes accuracy, the ability to sense what is beneath the surface. Wisdom refuses to skate across the surface and ignore what is deep within. It penetrates.

2. "By *understanding* it is established. . . ."

Understanding is responding with insight. Instead of fighting back and taking comments personally, understanding insightfully weighs things with perspective.

3. "By *knowledge* the rooms are filled with all precious and pleasant riches."

Knowledge is learning with perception. It includes things like a teachable spirit, a willingness to listen, a desire to discover . . . to find out what is really there. Knowledge forever pursues the truth.

So much for the basic building materials every home must have. What about the results? What happens when wisdom, understanding, and knowledge team up and go to work? Again . . . three results are spelled out by Solomon, each corresponding to a separate "ingredient." You will notice that these words have nothing to do with physical materials or tangible creature comforts. A home doesn't have to have a two-car garage or a matching sofa and chair in the living room or wall-to-wall carpet. What is essential? Wisdom, understanding, and knowledge.

1. By wisdom a house is *built* (v. 3).

The Hebrew term for built suggests "to restore." It is the idea of *re*building something so that it flourishes once again.

2. By understanding it is *established* (v. 3).

The word translated "established" means "set in order." It's the idea of putting something back into an upright position . . . something that was once leaning, falling, or twisted.

3. By knowledge the rooms are *filled* with all precious and pleasant riches (v. 4).

When Solomon wrote "by knowledge the home is *filled,*" he used a term that meant fulfillment, ever-abundant satisfaction. The constant pursuit of the truth makes that happen. And those "precious and pleasant riches"? Those would be the things that last. To name a few: happy memories, positive and wholesome attitudes, feelings of affirmation, acceptance, and esteem, mutual respect, good relationships, and depth of character.

Sounds so wonderful, doesn't it? Almost too ideal to be possible? No, God never dangles theoretical carrots in front of us, mocking us with unattainable possibilities.

Is your home beginning to deteriorate? Are those living in the home lacking a team spirit, a mutual commitment to relationships? Since you cannot force others to change, start with yourself. Begin to demonstrate those three ingredients that have the ability to transform a house virtually in shambles into a home of purpose and harmony.

Yes . . . start with yourself.

EFLECTIONS
ON DOMESTIC
DISHARMONY

1. Write out Proverbs 24:3–4 on some paper in your own handwriting. Tape the piece of paper onto your bathroom mirror. Since the words flow rather easily, commit them to memory this week. Each morning and each evening, as you review those thoughts, tell the Lord you want them to become a reality in your home. Ask Him to show you ways you can demonstrate wisdom; understanding, and knowledge. Don't make a public announcement of your plan, just begin quietly. Stay at it.

2. As you drive (or walk) home each evening this week, mentally prepare yourself for whatever you may have to face. Remind yourself to remain calm and considerate, nondefensive, cooperative, and thoughtful. Each day this week do something (or *say* something) that will encourage each member of your family. Watch the Lord honor your unselfishness. It may be remarkable how He begins to lift you beyond your daily grind of domestic disharmony.

3. Perhaps you now live alone . . . but you learned many of these principles from both your parents or one of them. Before the week has ended, write or call. Express your gratitude for the things you learned. Be specific as you state your appreciation. You may even add a few lines you read from this section of the book as you describe why you are so thankful.

TRANSITION

Congratulations! You have not only finished the first twenty-six weeks of our readings and reflections in the songs and sayings of Scripture, you have reached the halfway mark in our year together. It has been quite a journey, hasn't it? You have faced some tough issues head on, and you have come to terms with several areas of your life that have needed attention. Good for you!

Our studies these past weeks have not been simple projects, but rather searching ones. That's the way God planned it. The songs of David and the sayings of Solomon were never meant to be shallow little jingles or cute and clever axioms. With inspired persuasion, they push their way into our life, they probe the secret recesses of our heart . . . they refuse to be ignored. As Scripture states, "There is no creature hidden from His sight, but all things are open and laid bare to the eyes of Him with whom we have to do" (Heb. 4:13).

As helpful as these weeks together may have been, our journey is incomplete. We have *another* twenty-six weeks to go! We need to return to those songs and, again, listen to the sweet singers of Israel. Their compositions await more of our time and attention; and, finally, we want to hear more counsel from the wise king whose proverbs provide the oil we need to handle life's demanding grinds.

Let me encourage you to start at the beginning of Book II with renewed determination and strong reliance on our heavenly Father. Living beyond the daily grind calls for both. I commend you for staying with me to the midway point. I think you will find the latter half of the journey just as rewarding and adventuresome as the former—maybe more!

And now . . . let's press on with fresh confidence and hope.

NOTES

Introduction

1. "Without a Song" words and music by Edward Eliscu, William Rose and Vincent Youmans. Copyright © 1929 (renewed 1957) Miller Music Corporation and Vincent Youmans Co., Inc. Published by Miller Music Corporation by arrangement with Vincent Youmans Co., Inc. All Rights of Miller Music Corporation assigned to SBK Catalogue Partnership. All rights administered by SBK Miller Catalog and Vincent Youmans Co., Inc. International copyright secured. Made in USA. All rights reserved. Used by Permission.

Section One

1. Joseph M. Scriven [1855], "What a Friend We Have in Jesus."
2. Immanuel Kant, *Critique of Practical Reason* [1781].
3. F. B. Meyer, *The Shepherd Psalm* (Grand Rapids, MI: Fleming H. Revell Company, 1895), 26.
4. Haddon W. Robinson, *The Good Shepherd,* formerly *Psalm Twenty-Three* (Chicago: Moody Press, 1968), 23.
5. Charles W. Slemming, *He Leadeth Me, The Shepherd's Life in Palestine* (Fort Washington, PA: Christian Literature Crusade, 1964), 64 pages.
6. Haddon W. Robinson, *The Good Shepherd,* 52.
7. F. B. Meyer, *The Shepherd Psalm,* 162.
8. Haddon W. Robinson, *The Good Shepherd,* 59.
9. J. Oswald Sanders, *Spiritual Leadership* (Chicago: Moody Press, 1967), 141.
10. Dr. and Mrs. Howard Taylor, *Hudson Taylor's Spiritual Secret* (Chicago, IL: Moody Press, 1958), 107.
11. George Keith [1787], "How Firm a Foundation."
12. Arthur Porritt, *John Henry Jowett* (London: Hodder and Stoughton, 1924), 290.
13. George Matheson [1882], "O Love That Will Not Let Me Go."
14. George W. Robinson [1838–1877], "Loved with Everlasting Love."
15. Martin Luther [1529], "A Mighty Fortress Is Our God"; translated by Frederick H. Hedge [1852].
16. Charles Schulz, "Peanuts" (New York: United Media). Copyright by Charles Schulz.
17. From *If* by Amy Carmichael. Copyright 1938 Dohnavur Fellowship (London: S.P.C.K.; Fort Washington, PA: Christian Literature Crusade). Used by permission.